Kaffe Fassett's
QUILTS in AMERICA

Designs inspired by vintage quilts from the American Museum in Britain

featuring
Liza Prior Lucy and Brandon Mably

The Taunton Press

First published in the USA in 2018 by

The Taunton Press
Inspiration for hands-on living®

The Taunton Press, Inc., 63 South Main Street,
PO Box 5506, Newtown, CT 06470-5506
email: tp@taunton.com

Patchwork designs	Kaffe Fassett, Liza Prior Lucy, Brandon Mably
Quilt making coordination	Heart Space Studios (Janet Haigh, Julie Harvey, Ilaria Padovani)
Technical editor	Lin Clements
Quilting	Judy Irish, Mary-Jane Hutchinson and Vickie Farrall
Designer	Anne Wilson
Art direction/styling	Kaffe Fassett
Location photography	Debbie Patterson
Stills photography	Steven Wooster
Illustrations	Heart Space Studios
Publishing consultant	Susan Berry (Berry & Co)

Library of Congress Cataloging-in-Publication Data
in progress

ISBN 978-1-63186-961-7

Colour reproduction	XY Digital, London

Printed in China

Page 1: My *Badge of Honour* quilt: an eye-catching
little log cabin design taken from the antique *Log
Cabin Quilt* in the American Museum in Bath.
Right: Liza's *Coleus Columns* redesign of the original
Nine-Patch Strip Quilt found the perfect setting on this
moss-covered barn.

Contents

introduction

I have thought about this book for years. Liza Lucy, who co-authors my hardback books, lives in a charming corner of Pennsylvania. On my many trips to work with her on quilts, we would drive through her neighbourhood, spotting locations that could showcase a quilt.

One day back in London, my team of Brandon, Susan and myself decided that our next book should be based on the gorgeous quilt collection at the American Museum in Bath. Their quilts were collected in the early 1960s and had never been shown outside Britain. We felt that our take on these antiques, using the latest fabrics in the Kaffe Collective, and a few Artisan ones, would make a very special 20th anniversary edition in our series.

It turned out to be the most satisfying and creative of the books I've produced so far. The layouts of the antique quilts were thrilling to work from, and for the most part, I made my versions pretty much as the originals. As our great team of quilt makers were creatively and expertly bringing the quilts to life, we began wondering where to photograph them. I knew Liza's historic New England-type setting would be just perfect to show off these early-American inspired quilts.

When Debbie Patterson, our intrepid English photographer, flew in to America to shoot the quilts, Brandon, Liza and I drove her around to the many barns, farmsteads and charming old houses we had

dreamed of using for years. The next day we started shooting in earnest but, in a week of abnormally hot autumn weather, we found the daytime sunlight too harsh for the intricate colours of our quilts, so we had to wait until evening to continue. Fortunately, the following day we were blessed with a soft, overcast day and were able to get some of our best shots. At each house and barn we chose, when we asked permission to photograph, the owners instantly agreed, making our job so much easier. You can see what stunning backgrounds they made for the quilts.

People might be surprised at the antique texture of many of the houses and barns we chose for the book. To me, much of America is very well kept, and even 100-year-old buildings look quite pristine in their newly painted state, so we searched for farms and houses with the weathered patina that looks best with our quilts. I have a particular love of working buildings that show a sense of history, along with the hard work that goes on in them, so this shoot was enormously satisfying for me.

Peaceable Farm

the original antique quilts

Here are the quilts in the American Museum collection from which Kaffe, with his team of designer/makers, drew inspiration for the 20 quilt designs in this book. Two quilts, the Nine-Patch Strip (page 17) and the Nine-Patch (page 14), each have an additional colourway. Each original quilt is given its date (if known) and a brief description, and is cross-referenced to its new design in the Gallery.

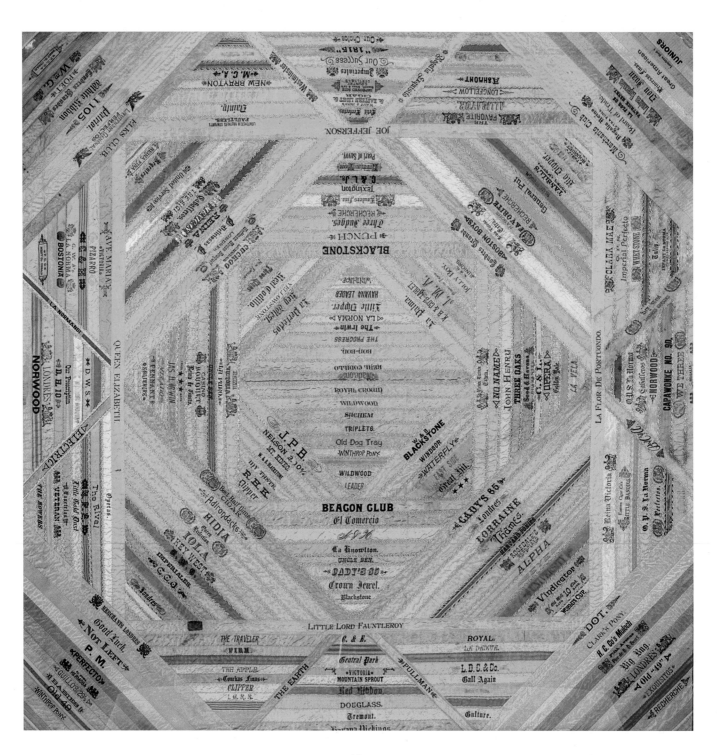

Log Cabin Quilt – Light and Dark Variation ►

Date: 1850–1899
Maker: Mrs. H. A. Batchelor
Size: 66in x 66in (163cm x 163cm)

One half of each block has been pieced in black silk so that when the blocks were set together a black star alternates with a coloured one. There is no quilting, so probably this piece of needlework was used as a sofa throw.
See *Badge of Honour* pp 26–7.

◄ Cigar Silk Ribbon Quilt Top

Date: c.1880
Maker: Unknown
Size: 41in x 41in (104cm x 104cm)

Cigar silk ribbons have been foundation-pieced to a backing fabric in the same manner as Log Cabin quilts. During the late 1800s, cigar companies tied bundles of cigars with silk ribbons, which had the name of the company or cigar manufacturer stamped on them. As cigar-smoking was a common activity, most households had a plentiful supply of these ribbons. The bright gold colour of these ribbons is still apparent in this piece. Yellow was the most common colour for the silk ribbons; different colours of ribbons denoted the different grades of cigars that were bound by them.
See *Red Ribbons* pp 40–41.

Quaker Square-in-a-Square Quilt ►

Date: 1835–1850
Maker: Made for the Yarnall family
Size: 84in x 96in (213cm x 244cm)

In this silk quilt in shades of fawn, brown, blue and gold, 42 Square-in-a-Square blocks have been joined together with striped fabric. The quilt belonged to a prominent Quaker family living in Pennsylvania, and it was probably made by the Yarnall family's sewing woman, mainly from pieces of silk left over from her dressmaking tasks.
See *Squares on Point* pp 30–31.

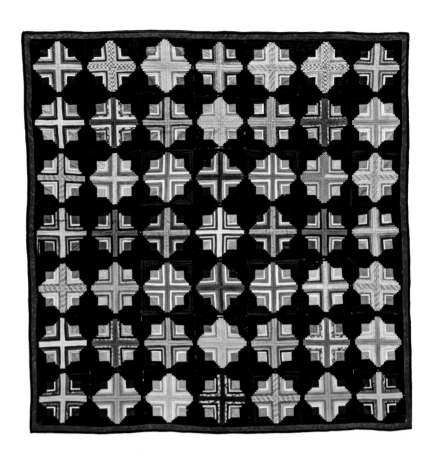

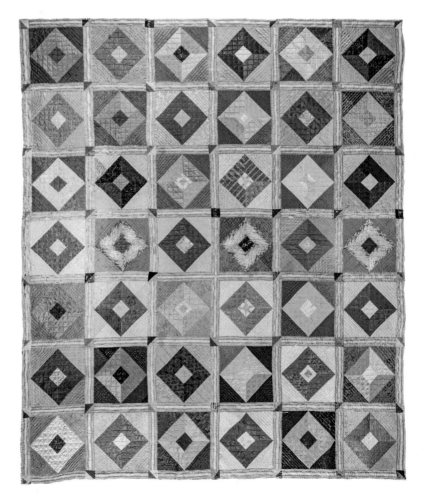

◄ *Mosaic Diamonds Quilt*

Date: 1861
Maker: Ann Eliza Urquhart
Size: 100in x 105in (254 x 267cm)

Cotton quilt top pieced from hexagons arranged in a repeating diamond pattern. Hexagons are one of the oldest known patchwork patterns, but in the 19th century they increased in popularity, as quilts using small hexagons were the ideal vehicle for showing off the new printed patterned fabrics that became available.
See *Green Boxes* pp 20–1.

◄ *Tumbling Blocks Star Quilt*

Date: 1852
Maker: Dr. Sarah Taylor Middleton Rogers
Size: 103in x 103in (255cm x 255cm)

This very large silk quilt has Tumbling Blocks sewn together in a Star formation. The entire Tumbling Blocks design is appliquéd onto a background of blue striped silk. Backed with bright blue glazed cotton, it was hand-quilted. It was made by Sarah Taylor Middleton (later Mrs. Rogers), a Quaker physician, for exhibition at the New Jersey State Fair, held in Trenton in 1852. The individual blocks have been arranged to form an eye-dazzling twelve-pointed star that creates optical illusions. Not surprisingly, the maker of this quilt won an award!
See *Giant Blocks* pp 22–3.

Sunburst Quilt ▶

Date: 1875–1899
Maker: Elizabeth Cannon Mitchell
Size: 65in x 72in (165cm x 183cm)

This variation of Star of Bethlehem is called
Sunburst and is pieced in the same way, with
each fabric diamond basted over paper before
being sewn together into the desired pattern.
The diamond arrangement terminates before
extending out into the (more customary) eight-
pointed star. As this design does not have large
points, the finished piece is smaller than is usual
for star quilts. The diamonds have been appliquéd
onto a yellow sateen background.
See *Starburst* pp 24–5.

Chintz Baskets Quilt ▶

Date: c.1850
Maker: Unknown
Size: 56¾in x 55½in (144cm x 141cm)
This small quilt was probably made as a lap quilt
or for a throw. The pieced basket blocks have been
sewn on point and have been divided with chintz
sashing. During construction, each of the blocks
has distorted slightly out of square. Upon sewing
the blocks together, this small error has been
magnified, resulting in the unusual shape of the
finished quilt.
See *Sashed Baskets* pp 58–9.

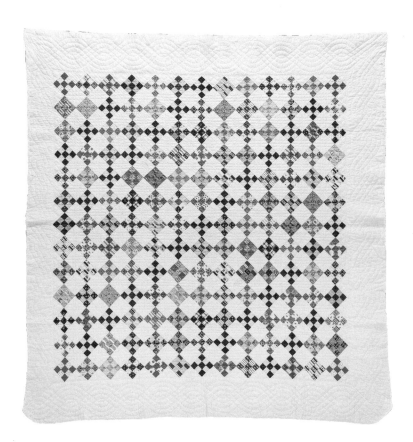

◄ *Nine-Patch Quilt*

Date: c.1850
Maker: Margaretta Boone Wintersteen
Size: 80in x 84in (203cm x 213cm)

A wide variety of early prints have been used to make the tiny squares that form the nine-patch blocks, which have been set diagonally (on point) and a definite colour scheme can be seen in the pattern.

The edges are turned in and finished with running stitch.
See *Kites* pp 34–5.

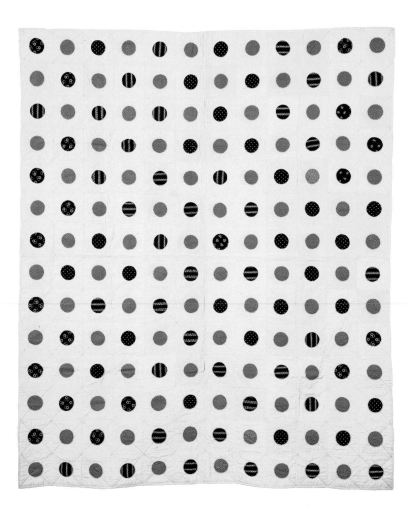

◄ *Baseballs Quilt*

Date: Late 19th century
Maker: Unknown
Size: 64¾in x 76½in (164cm x 194cm)

Small circles of patterned red and blue cotton, representing baseballs, have been appliquéd onto squares of unbleached calico. The circles are surrounded with chain stitch worked in coarse cotton yarn, and chain stitch is also worked diagonally across the intersections of the blocks. There is outline quilting round the circles and on either side of the chain-stitch diagonals. Four hearts have bren embroidered in the centre.
See *Technicolour Circles* pp 54–5.

Friendship Quilt – Star Variation ▶

Date: 1847
Maker: St. George's Church congregation
Size: 99in x 99in (251cm x 251cm)

A selection of red and white printed calicos was used to make over 100 eight-pointed star blocks. Many of the white background squares and circular star centres are signed and dated. Two rows of red triangles, facing inwards, form the border.

Signature quilts using a repeated block design to create a pattern over the quilt top are called Friendship quilts (distinguishing them from the elaborately appliquéd Album quilts). The fashion for Signature quilts originated in Pennsylvania and Maryland in the early 1840s.
See *Red Stars* pp 32–3.

Silk Square-in-a-Square Quilt ▶

Date: 1875–1885
Maker: Unknown
Size: 55in x 60¼in (140cm x 153cm)

The vibrant colours of the fabrics used in the Square-in-a-Square blocks zing out from the black satin sashing that frames them. The quilt is made from silks and velvets that have been carefully cut so that the stripes in the triangles line up across the blocks and the floral motifs are centred in the middle of the square patches. A dark purple satin border frames the quilt.
See *Moonlight* pp 50–51.

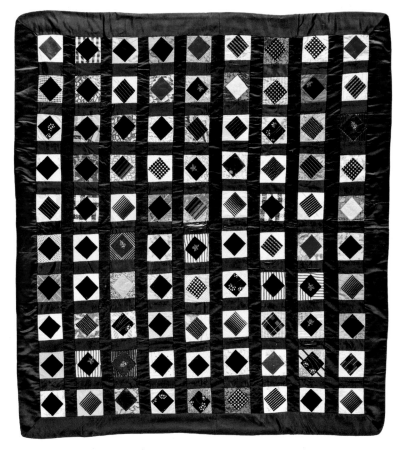

◄ *Hexagonal Star Quilt Top*

Date: 1880–1890
Maker: Unknown
Size: 69in x 63in (175cm x 160cm)

In this quilt, hexagonal shapes cut from tie silks have been pieced to make further hexagons, linked by small black silk diamonds. The border (which was added later) is of navy blue silk patterned with white. This quilt top has never been backed or quilted, and all piecing was done by hand over papers.
See *Bold Hexagons* pp 52–3.

◄ *Tippecanoe and Tyler Too Quilt*

Date: 1840–1849
Maker: Elizabeth Karen
Size: 74in x 80in (188cm x 203cm)

The white cotton blocks each contain an eight-pointed star of coloured fabrics. The blocks are set on point within an English chintz border, while the backing fabric is American printed cotton with a political theme from which the name of the quilt is drawn: "Tippecanoe and Tyler Too" was the title of a campaign song used by the Whigs during the 1840 presidential election. This must have been a much loved quilt because it has been re-stitched where worn areas were removed. It is clear that these repairs were made after the quilt was finished as the quilting is now interrupted by seams.
See *Tippecanoe and Tyler Too* pp 42–3.

Bridal Chest Quilt ▶

Date: c. 1832
Maker: Unknown Bride in Chester County,
Pennsylvania
Size: 102in x 91½in (259cm x 232cm)

Made by a bride of English descent living in
Chester County, Pennsylvania, this quilt is
constructed from thousands of pieces of decorated
cotton, printed in the early 19th century. Tiny
fabric squares are arranged in Nine-Patch blocks,
which flow in diagonal bands across the quilt.
The space in between is packed with triangles,
each filling half a square. Given the precision
of the piecing, the fabric squares were almost
certainly stitched over papers before being sewn
together. Remarkably, some of the tiny squares
are made from smaller scraps. The scrappy nature
of the quilt has been tempered by using only two
different fabrics in each Nine-Patch.
See *Autumn* pp 44–5.

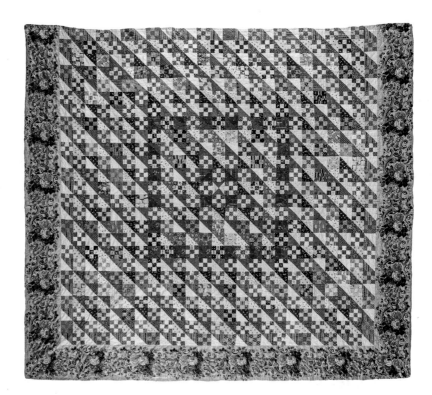

Nine-Patch Strip Quilt ▶

Date: 1817
Maker: SG
Size: 93in x 100in (236cm x 254cm)

Six columns of floral chintz alternate with five
bands of Nine-Patch blocks. Each of these blocks is
set on point within triangles of blue chintz. Backed
with muslin and bound with hand-woven tape,
Nine-Patch is an early patchwork block and often
forms the foundation for many later and more
complex designs. The European glazed cottons
featured on this quilt illustrate the crisp details
produced by copperplate printing processes
in the late eighteenth century. The columns of
straight chintz have been cut from the same fabric,
creating continuity in design.
See *Contrast Columns* pp 36–7 and *Coleus
Columns* pp 38–9.

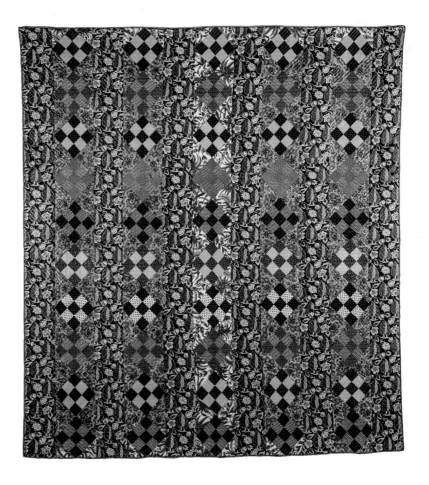

◄ Fan Quilt

Date: 1937
Maker: Katy Clark Elmore
Size: 79in x 86in (201cm x 208cm)

Pieced fans in multi-coloured cottons are set on a white background, to make square blocks set diamond-wise. The quilt has a white cotton backing and is outline quilted. The quilt edge is bound in striped cotton and the upper edge is scalloped.
See *Dotty Fans* pp 56–7.

Log Cabin Quilt – Barn Raising Variation (backing) ►

Date: 1863–1886
Makers: Ellen Bryant Smith and Sarah Bryant
Size: 76in x 80in (193cm x 203cm)

Narrow cotton strips were used to construct the basic Log Cabin blocks on the front of the quilt by Ellen Bryant, while the backing (the inspiration for the modern version in this book) was made by her sister, Sarah, and is also pieced, with 60 squares created from minute scraps of different cottons, cut into half-square triangles, divided by floral printed cotton sashing. The quilt is bound with red cotton.

There is no quilting, nor has the quilt been tied, which has caused some minor structural distortion.
See *Stonewall* pp 28–9.

◄ Nine-Patch Scrap Quilt

Date: 19th century
Maker: Unknown
Size: 85in x 90in (216cm x 229cm)

Various printed cottons have been pieced together to make this version of a Nine-Patch top. Brown and white checked cotton has been used for the backing. The quilting is in straight lines, and the quilt is bound in blue and white checked cotton. This is a quilt where pieces from the family scrap bag may have been used to make the top.
See *Pastel Nine-Patch* pp 46–7 and *Dark Nine-Patch* pp 48–9.

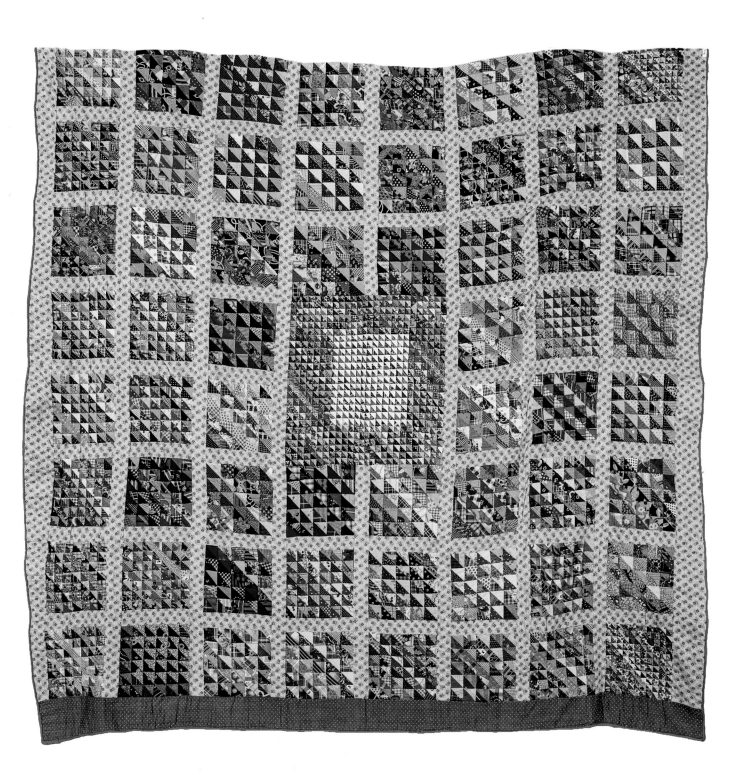

Green Boxes
by Kaffe Fassett

Tumbling Blocks have always been a favourite of mine. I've done them in knitting patterns and needlepoints, and have even painted a floor in this classic pattern. Here I've used mostly soft Spring shades of green to go with this charming Victorian house.
See *Mosaic Diamonds Quilt*, page 12.

OVERLEAF

Giant Blocks
by Kaffe Fassett

The Quaker quilt that inspired this design is an appliquéd star, but I used the centre of the star for my redesign as I felt it made a powerful enough statement on its own. I love the colours of this piece.
See *Tumbling Blocks Star Quilt*, page 12.

Starburst
by Kaffe Fassett

Instead of a round Sunburst
pattern, I created this strong
pointed star, which has a
more dynamic effect. I love
the lacelike quality of the
colours in the original quilt,
so went for a soft pastel
palette of prints.
See *Sunburst Quilt*, page 13.

Badge of Honour
by Kaffe Fassett

This is the most intricate of our quilts. Since I was so impressed at the organization of the original, I tried to make sure mine was as close in mood as possible. I like the patriotic contrast palette.
See *Log Cabin Quilt – Light and Dark Variation*, page 11.

Stonewall
by Kaffe Fassett

I loved the intricate points in the backing of the original quilt and chose to reproduce this in my redesign. I only realized that the colours in each block repeated diagonally once I sat down to organize my version.
See *Log Cabin Quilt – Barn Raising Variation (backing)*, page 19.

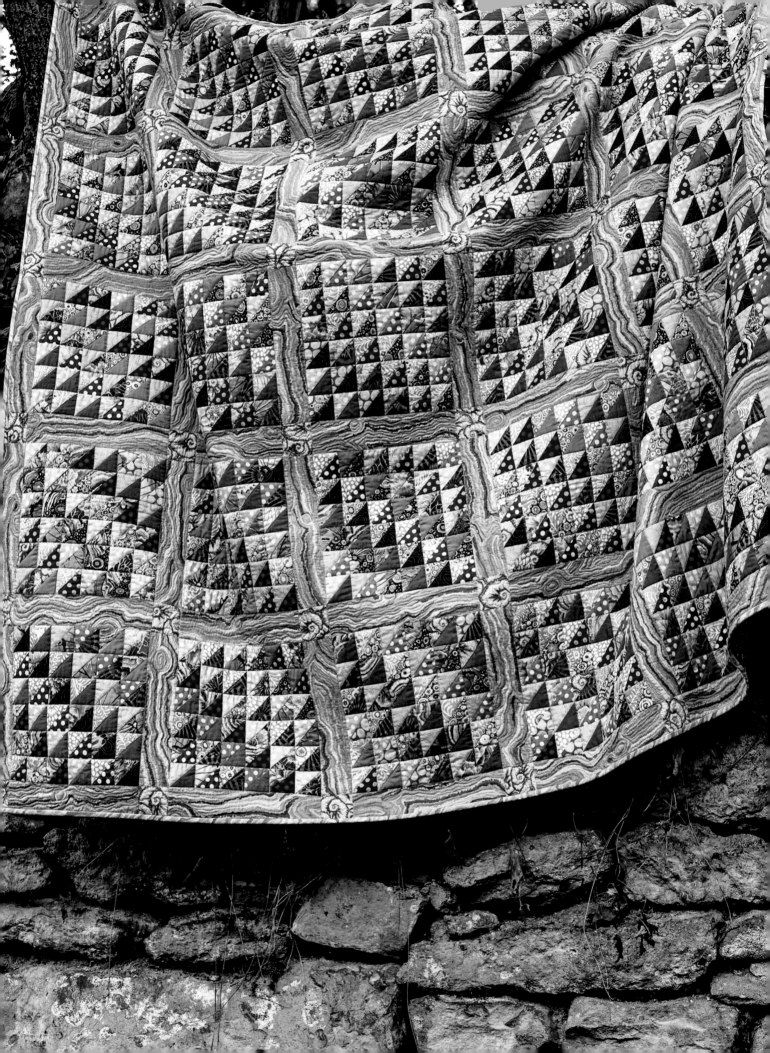

Squares on Point
by Kaffe Fassett

Another Quaker quilt as inspiration. I love the simple layout, which shows off our large prints so elegantly.
See *Quaker Square-in-a-Square Quilt*, page 11.

Red Stars
by Kaffe Fassett

For my take on this quilt, I softened the sharp contrast of the original red and white fabrics by placing my red stars on a Spot fabric background in duck-egg blue.
See *Friendship Quilt – Star Variation*, page 15.

Kites
by Kaffe Fassett

The kaleidoscopic nature of the sharp, bright colours on the pale ground of the original quilt attracted me as it is so deliciously different from the rest of the quilts in the Museum's collection. If I were doing this again, though, I'd leave off the pale border, making the colours sing out more. See *Nine-Patch Quilt*, page 14.

Contrast Columns
by Kaffe Fassett

I just love these two very different but equally bold designs that show off the upscale prints so well. My version here uses our black and white Vine fabric for the single fabric columns.
See *Nine-Patch Strip Quilt*, page 17.

OVERLEAF

Coleus Columns
by Liza Prior Lucy

In Liza's version of the same quilt, the autumnal hues are so atuned to the landscape colours that the quilt almost disappears on this old shed.

Red Ribbons
by Kaffe Fassett

In the original quilt, based on yellow cigar ribbons, I loved the way the writing on the labels was lined up. We tried to replicate that patterned look using closely toned, hot-coloured prints. See *Cigar Silk Ribbon Quilt Top*, page 10.

Tippecanoe and Tyler Too
by Liza Prior Lucy

Liza has created a rich interpretation of this quilt using just three fabrics – my multi stripes are the perfect choice for the various stars, cleverly cut to make them appear to swirl. The purple porch with its dark green rocking chairs is just the setting for it.

See *Tippecanoe and Tyler Too Quilt*, page 16.

Autumn
by Kaffe Fassett

I was attracted to the strong diagonals in this quilt. It is yet another use of the ingenious nine-patch block. See *Bridal Chest Quilt*, page 17.

Pastel Nine-Patch
by Kaffe Fassett

It was the odd layout for this nine-patch quilt that first
attracted my eye. It was fun to see how it behaved in the two
different versions – one in sugary pastels, shown here, and
the other in rich dark fabrics (see overleaf).
See *Nine-Patch Scrap Quilt*, page 18.

Dark Nine-Patch
Brandon Mably

Brandon put his version of this design together using many
of his new prints. The rich dark colours really glowed in the
American autumn light. I think the rusted old railroad carriage
really sets it off too.
See *Nine-Patch Scrap Quilt*, page 18.

Moonlight
by Kaffe Fassett

I loved the challenge of creating this beauty in the darkest colours we produce to echo the wonderful rich coloured satins, silks and velvets of the original. See *Silk Square-in-a-Square Quilt*, page 15.

Bold Hexagons
by Liza Prior Lucy

Isn't this purple Victorian house the perfect setting for the glowing palette of Liza's quilt? Frenchtown, in New Jersey, where we found this bed and breakfast, is known for its coloured houses.
Hexagonal Star Quilt Top, page 16.

Technicolour Circles
by Kaffe Fassett

Baseballs – the original quilt with dark circles on a cream ground – has been given a new twist in my version of it. Using a black Spot ground fabric (instead of the cream) gave me the idea to go for a wide palette of bright tones for the balls themselves. See *Baseballs Quilt*, page 14.

Dotty Fans
by Kaffe Fassett

I have always liked fan quilts. I noticed that the bits I liked best on the fans in the original quilt were polka dots, so I opted for many different colours of spotted fabrics in my version.
See *Fan Quilt*, page 18.

Sashed Baskets
by Kaffe Fassett

My Paint Pots fabric creates
abstract flowers or fruits
while the Gerbera print in
blue and white creates a
fresh-looking basket, but my
favourite thing in this quilt
is the sashing in Brandon's
Shark's Teeth fabric.
See *Chintz Baskets Quilt*,
page 13.

stonewall **

Kaffe Fassett

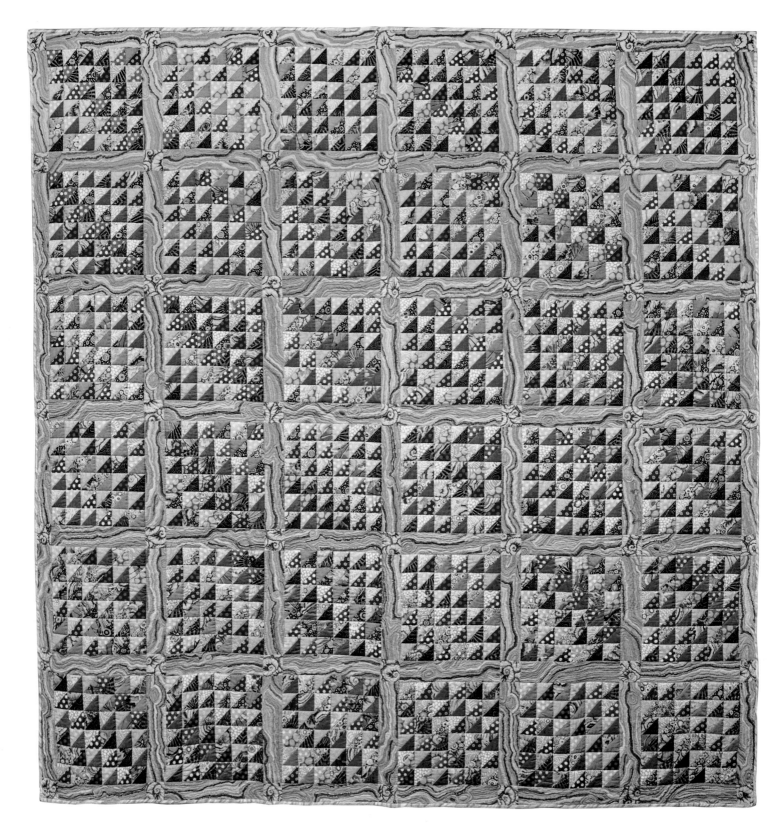

This quilt is scrappy but organized, with the darks and lights carefully arranged in diagonal "rows" within each block, but it doesn't matter which of the given fabrics you choose for each of the rows. There is no need to place each fabric as in the original.

Just be sure to use only one light and one dark for each diagonal "row" in each block. Also note that some of the fabrics can be used as either darks or lights, depending on the fabric with which they are paired.

SIZE OF FINISHED QUILT
89½in x 89½in (227.3cm x 227.3cm)

MATERIALS
Fabrics calculated at minimum width of 40in (101.6cm) and are cut across the width, unless otherwise stated

Patchwork and Border Fabrics
JUPITER
Stone   GP131ST   2½yds (2.3m)
CURLIQUE
Grey   PJ87GY   ¾yd (70cm)

Light Fabrics
½yd (45cm) each of the following:
FERNS
Yellow   GP147YE
Grey   GP147GY
PAPERWEIGHT
Sludge   GP20SL
ABORIGINAL DOT
Silver   GP71SV
GUINEA FLOWER
Grey   GP59GY
BRASSICA
Grey   PJ51GY
SPOT
Duck egg   GP70DE
Silver   GP70SV
TREE FUNGI
Grey   PJ82GY

Dark Fabrics
½yd (45cm) each of the following:
SPOT
Brown   GP70BR
Charcoal   GP70CRC
Cocoa   GP70CC
PAPERWEIGHT
Grey   GP20GY
ROMAN GLASS
Byzantine   GP01BY
ABORIGINAL DOT
Chocolate   GP71CL
LOTUS LEAF
Mauve   GP29MV
BRASSICA
Dark   PJ51DK
PAPER FANS
Black   GP143BK

SHOT COTTON
Smoky   SC20
Pewter   SC22

Both Light and Dark Fabrics
½yd (45cm) each of the following:
JUMBLE
Turquoise   BM53TQ
SPOT
Storm   GP70SM
SHOT COTTON
Galvanized SC87

Backing Fabric
ROMAN GLASS
Byzantine   GP01BY   7yd (6.4m)

Binding
JUPITER
Grey   GP131GY   1yd (90cm)

Batting
98in x 98in (249cm x 249cm)

Quilting Thread
Machine quilting thread

CUTTING OUT

Remove selvedges from all fabrics before you cut.

Sashing Strips

Cut 84 rectangles from GP131ST, each 3in x 12½in (7.6cm x 31.8cm). Note that the stripe pattern runs across the width of the fabric so the stripes will run parallel to the long edges of the rectangles.

Corner Posts

Cut 49 squares from PJ87GY, each 3in x 3in (7.6cm x 7.6cm). Use the rest of this fabric as a *light* fabric for half-square triangles.

Half-square Triangles

Cut all the rest of the fabric into half-square triangles by cutting squares each 2⅞in x 2⅞in (7.3cm x 7.3cm). Cut each square once diagonally to make 2 triangles from each square. You will need a total of 1,296 light triangles and 1,296 dark triangles. In the beginning, it is best to cut each block as you go.

Backing

Cut 2 lengths each approx. 98in (249cm) long from GP01BY. From the remaining fabric cut 2 rectangles 19in (48.3cm) wide x 49½in (125.7cm) long.

Binding

Cut 2½in (6.4cm) wide strips of GP131GY on the bias, sufficient to make a binding length of at least 370in (940m) long.

Tip

Although I don't recommend it in my workshops, If you need a faster method of making half-square triangle units (making 2 at once), then don't cut the squares into triangles. Instead, place a light and dark square right sides together, mark the diagonal line and then sew ¼in (6mm) away from both sides of the line. Cut apart on the line and press the 2 units open.

BLOCK ASSEMBLY DIAGRAM

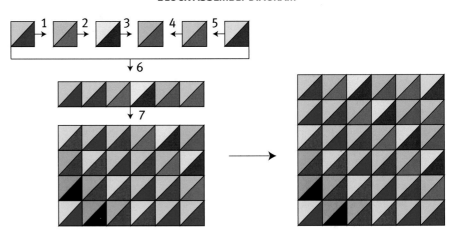

MAKING THE BLOCKS

Use a ¼in (6mm) seam allowance throughout.

For every square in the blocks, pair a light triangle with a dark triangle and sew together on their long diagonal edges to make 1 half-square triangle (HST) unit (a two-tone square).

Each block comprises 36 HST units, which are sewn together in 6 horizontal rows of 6 HST units each (see Block Assembly Diagram). Follow the diagram carefully to create the effect of diagonal rows of HSTs, with the dark triangle always at bottom right of an HST unit. The units in each diagonal "row" are made from the same two fabrics, i.e. the same light fabric and the same dark fabric.

Make 36 blocks in total.

MAKING THE QUILT

Lay out the blocks in a 6 x 6 arrangement to your liking, making sure all the blocks are in the same orientation. Sew the blocks together into horizontal rows with a vertical sashing strip between each block and at each end of each row (see Quilt Assembly Diagram). Make 6 block rows.

For each row of horizontal sashing, take 6 horizontal sashing strips and sew them together with a corner post between each strip and at each end of each row. Make 7 sashing rows.

Sew the block rows together with a sashing row between them and at the top and bottom of the quilt top.

FINISHING THE QUILT

Press the quilt top. Using a ¼in (6mm) seam allowance, sew the narrow rectangles of backing fabric together end to end to make a strip approx. 98in (249cm) long x 19in (48.3cm) wide. Sew this strip between the larger pieces of backing fabric to make a backing approx. 98in x 98in (249cm x 249cm).

Layer the quilt top, batting and backing, and then baste together (see page 164). Quilt as preferred. The quilt shown was quilted in the ditch around all of the triangles. The border was quilted with random ripple patterns that loosely follow the fabric design.

Trim the quilt edges and attach the binding (see page 165).

QUILT ASSEMBLY DIAGRAM

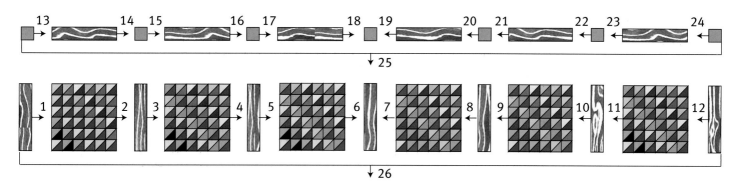

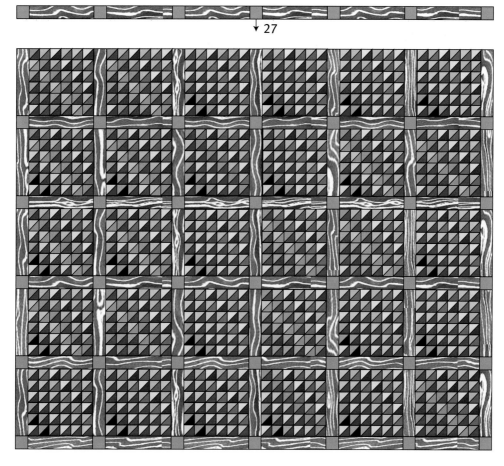

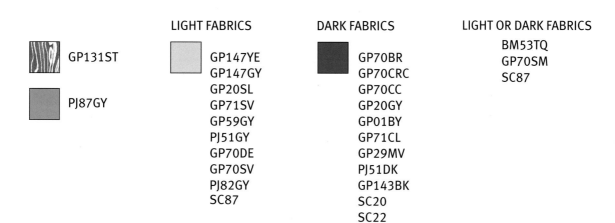

LIGHT FABRICS

GP147YE
GP147GY
GP20SL
GP71SV
GP59GY
PJ51GY
GP70DE
GP70SV
PJ82GY
SC87

DARK FABRICS

GP70BR
GP70CRC
GP70CC
GP20GY
GP01BY
GP71CL
GP29MV
PJ51DK
GP143BK
SC20
SC22

LIGHT OR DARK FABRICS

BM53TQ
GP70SM
SC87

GP131ST

PJ87GY

squares on point **

Kaffe Fassett

Colourful square-within-a-square blocks create the on-point layout for this quilt. The sashing is cut to showcase the zig zag pattern of the fabric both horizontally and vertically, combined with bright corner posts in Spot fabric.

SIZE OF FINISHED QUILT
75in x 89½in (190.5cm x 227cm)

MATERIALS
Fabrics calculated at minimum width of 40in (101.6cm) and are cut across the width, unless otherwise stated

Patchwork Fabrics
ZIG ZAG
Black   BM43BK   2⅛yd (2m)

1¼yd (1.2m) each of the following:
ABORIGINAL DOT
Forest   GP71FO
MILLEFIORE
Antique   GP92AN

½yd (45cm) each of the following:
JAPANESE CHRYSANTHEMUM
Antique   PJ41AN
VINE
Royal   GP151RY
DREAM
Dark   GP148DK
HORSE CHESTNUT
Brown   PJ84BR
BRASSICA
Purple   PJ51PU
SOUND WAVES
Green   BM62GN

⅜yd (35cm) each of the following:
SPOT
Royal   GP70RY
Black   GP70BK

¼yd (25cm) each of the following:
PAPER FANS
Black   GP143BK
HORSE CHESTNUT
Red   PJ84RD
Blue   PJ84BL
LOTUS LEAF
Umber   GP29UM
GLORY
Dark   PJ85DK
JAPANESE CHRYSANTHEMUM
Red   PJ41RD

Backing Fabric
SPIRAL SHELLS
Antique   PJ73AN   6½yd (6.5m)

Binding
ZIG ZAG
Black   BM43BK   ¾yd (70cm)

Batting
83in x 98in (211cm x 249cm)

Quilting Thread
Machine quilting thread

CUTTING OUT
Remove selvedges from all fabrics before cutting. Measurements include a seam allowance of ¼in (6mm) unless otherwise stated.

Sashing Strips
Cut BM43BK with the zig zag pattern running across the width of the fabric (selvedge to selvedge). Cut 71 rectangles, each 3in x 12½in (7.6cm x 31.8cm). The zig zag pattern direction will thus be horizontal for the horizontal sashing strips and vertical for the vertical sashing strips (exactly as in the Sashing Strip Stripe Direction Diagram below).

SASHING STRIP STRIPE DIRECTION DIAGRAM

Zig zag direction for horizontal sashing

Zig zag direction for vertical sashing ⟶

Corner Posts
From GP70RY cut 42 squares 3in x 3in (7.6cm x 7.6cm).

Block Backgrounds
From GP71FO cut 30 squares 6⅞in x 6⅞in (17.5cm x 17.5cm). Cut each square diagonally once to make 2 triangles (for a total of 60 triangles). From GP92AN cut 30 squares 6⅞in x 6⅞in (17.5cm x 17.5cm). Cut each square diagonally once to make 2 triangles (for a total of 60 triangles).

Block Centres
From GP70BK cut 120 squares 2in x 2in (5cm x 5cm).
From the remaining fabrics, cut the following number of 6⅞in x 6⅞in (17.5cm x 17.5cm) squares and cut each square diagonally once to make 2 triangles, as follows:
PJ41AN, 6 squares (12 triangles); GP151RY, 6 squares (12 triangles); GP148DK, 6 squares (12 triangles); PJ84BR, 6 squares (12 triangles); PJ51PU, 6 squares (12 triangles); BM62GN,

6 squares (12 triangles); GP143BK, 4 squares (8 triangles); PJ84RD, 4 squares (8 triangles); GP29UM, 4 squares (8 triangles); PJ85DK, 4 squares (8 triangles); PJ41RD, 4 squares (8 triangles) and PJ84BL, 4 squares (8 triangles).

Backing
From PJ73AN cut 2 lengths 98in (249cm) long and 3 strips 5in x 33in (12.7cm x 83.8cm).

Binding
In BM43BK cut 2½in (6.4cm) wide strips on the bias, sufficient to make a binding length of at least 340in (864cm).
JH: Check if bias cut.

MAKING THE BLOCKS
Use a ¼in (6mm) seam allowance throughout.
Make each block with 4 identical background triangles, 4 identical centre triangles plus 4 squares of GP70BK. Follow the Unit Assembly Diagram for making up each unit and the Block Assembly Diagram for making up a block.

MAKING THE QUILT
Lay out the blocks, alternating the two background colours and interspacing them with the sashing strips and corner posts as shown in the Quilt Assembly Diagram, joining into rows (i.e. 6 rows of blocks and 7 rows of sashing strips), then join the rows to complete the quilt top.

FINISHING THE QUILT
Press the quilt top. Using a ¼in (6mm) seam allowance, sew the 3 narrow pieces of backing together end to end. Sew this narrow panel between the two larger backing pieces to form a piece approx. 84in x 98in (213.4cm x 249cm).
Layer the quilt top, batting and backing, and baste together (see page 164). Quilt as preferred. The quilt shown was quilted in the ditch around the large and small diamonds. The sashing was quilted with occasional outline zig zag patterns following the fabric design.
Trim the quilt edges and attach the binding (see page 165).

UNIT ASSEMBLY DIAGRAM

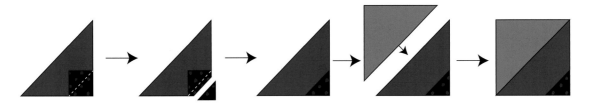

BLOCK ASSEMBLY DIAGRAM

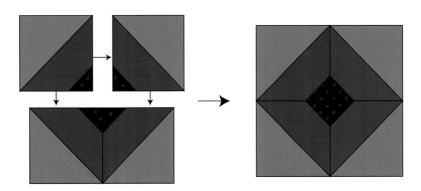

QUILT ASSEMBLY DIAGRAM

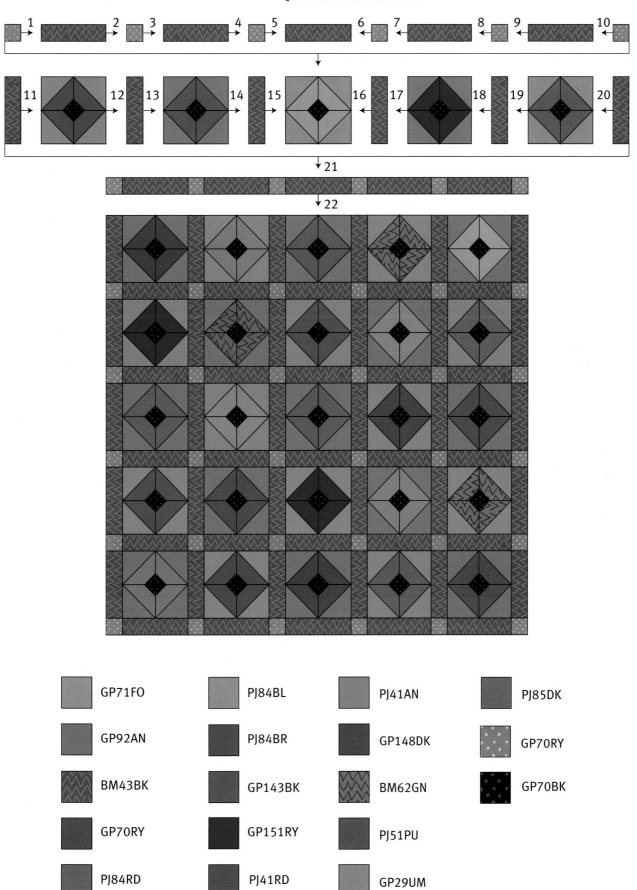

	GP71FO		PJ84BL		PJ41AN		PJ85DK
	GP92AN		PJ84BR		GP148DK		GP70RY
	BM43BK		GP143BK		BM62GN		GP70BK
	GP70RY		GP151RY		PJ51PU		
	PJ84RD		PJ41RD		GP29UM		

kites **

Kaffe Fassett

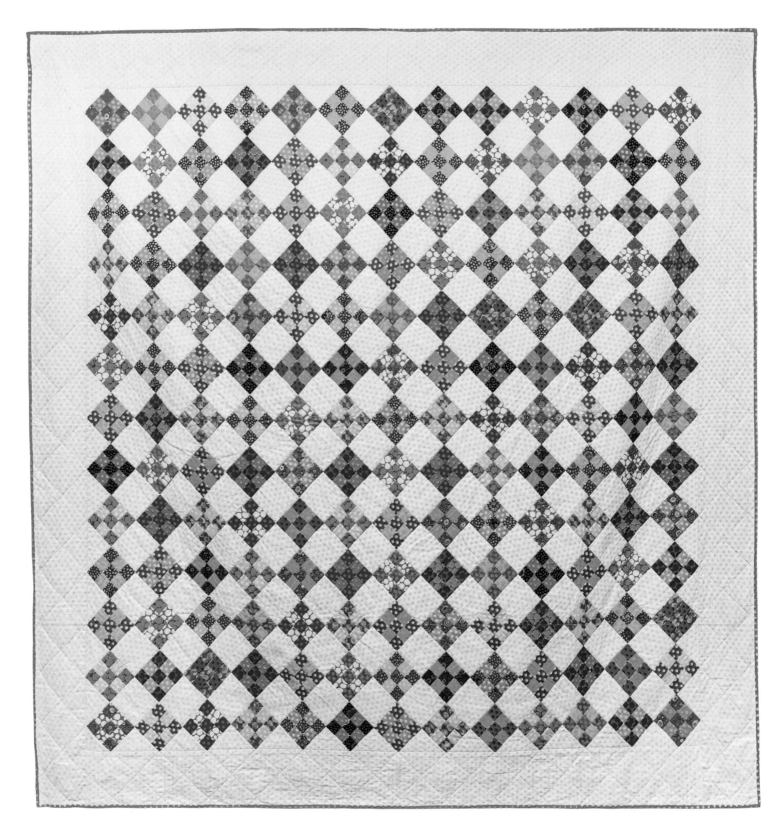

The 9-patch blocks on point appear to float in this design, thanks to the use of a single light Spot background fabric. Cutting and instructions are given for the quilt shown, but this is a scrappy-style quilt so it isn't necessary to place the fabrics or blocks exactly as in the original. However, for the checkerboard effect do maintain the light/dark balance of the blocks.

SIZE OF FINISHED QUILT
97in x 97in (246.4cm x 246.4cm)

MATERIALS
Fabrics calculated at minimum width of 40in (101.6cm) and are cut across the width, unless otherwise stated

Patchwork and Border Fabrics
SPOT

Soft Blue	GP70SF	5¼yd (4.8m)
Duck Egg	GP70DE	⅜yd (35cm)
Green	GP70GN	¼yd (25cm)
Peach	GP70PH	⅜yd (35cm)
Teal	GP70TE	½yd (45cm)
Ochre	GP70OC	⅜yd (35cm)
Apple	GP70AL	¼yd (25cm)
Lichen	GP70LN	¼yd (25cm)
Shocking	GP70SG	¼yd (25cm)
Sapphire	GP70SP	¼yd (25cm)

JUMBLE

Tangerine	BM53TN	⅜yd (35cm)
Candy	BM53CD	⅜yd (35cm)
Ocean	BM53ON	⅜yd (35cm)

BAUBLES

Red	BM61RD	⅜yd (35cm)

ABORIGINAL DOT

Lime	GP71LM	⅜yd (35cm)

ROMAN GLASS

Red	GP01RD	⅜yd (35cm)

GUINEA FLOWER

Cobalt	GP59CB	⅜yd (35cm)
Purple	GP59PU	¼yd (25cm)

PAPERWEIGHT

Purple	GP20PU	¼yd (25cm)

Backing Fabric
CARPET

Pastel	GP001PT	3yd (2.75m)

of 108in (274cm) wide or 8⅛yd (7.5m) of standard width

Binding
SPOT

Shocking	GP70SG	⅞yd (80cm)

Batting
105in x 105in (266.7cm x 266.7cm)

Quilting Thread
Machine quilting thread

PATCHES
All patches include a ¼in (6mm) seam allowance.
Large squares for unpieced blocks: 5in x 5in (12.7cm x 12.7cm).
Small squares for 9-patch blocks: 2in x 2in (5cm x 5cm).
Side setting triangles: 7⅝in (19.4cm) square, cut into 4 triangles.
Corner triangles: 4in (10.2cm) square, cut into 2 triangles.

CUTTING OUT
Remove selvedges from all fabrics before cutting. Cut the border strips first from the *length* of fabric GP70SF. Cut all subsequent patches from the remaining fabric.

Border
From GP70SF and cutting from the *length* of the fabric, cut 2 strips 7½in x 83¼in (19cm x 211.5cm) for the top and bottom of the quilt. Cut 2 pieces 7½in x 97¼in (19cm x 247cm) for the sides of the quilt.

Large squares: From GP70SF cut strips 5in (12.7cm) across the remaining width of the fabric. Cut the strips into 5in (12.7cm) squares. Cut 144 squares in total.

Small squares: Cut strips 2in (5cm) wide across the full width of the fabric. Cut each strip into 2in (5cm) squares. Each strip will give you 20 squares. Cut the following numbers of squares (for a total of 1,521). GP70DE 92; GP70GN 50; GP70PH 100; GP70TE 130; GP70OC 104; GP70AL 56; GP70LN 75; GP70SG 76; GP70SP 70; BM53TN 108; BM53CD 112; BM53ON 90; BM61RD 95; GP71LM 88; GP01RD 100; GP59CB 105; GP59PU 35 and GP20PU 35.

Side setting triangles: From GP70SF cut strips 7⅝in (19.4cm) wide across the width of the remaining fabric. Cut each strip into 7⅝in (19.4cm) squares. Cut 12 squares and cut each square in half along both diagonals to give 4 triangles, for a total of 48 triangles.

Corner triangles: From the remainder of GP70SF cut 2 squares 4in (10.2cm). Cut each square once diagonally to give 2 triangles per square, for a total of 4 triangles.

Backing
If using extra-wide backing, cut a piece 105in x 105in (266.7cm x 266.7cm) in GP001PT.
If using standard-width backing, cut 2 pieces 40in x 105in (102cm x 266.7cm) and 3 pieces 40in x 26in (102cm x 66cm) in GP001PT. Join the 3 narrower pieces together end to end and trim to 105in (266.7cm) long.

Binding
From GP70SG cut 11 strips 2½in (6.4cm) x width of fabric.

Tip
The triangle patches have bias edges. Using spray starch prior to cutting will help stabilize them until they are sewn. Take care when handling and pressing.

BLOCK ASSEMBLY DIAGRAM

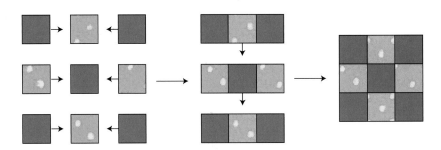

BLOCK COLOURWAYS DIAGRAM

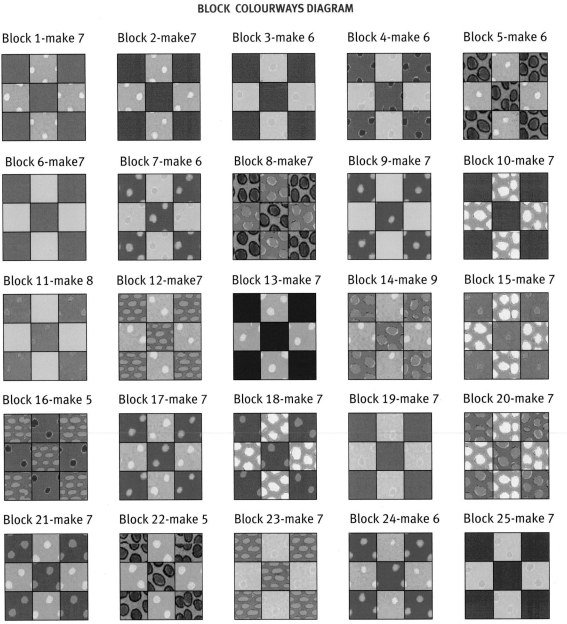

Block 1-make 7 Block 2-make7 Block 3-make 6 Block 4-make 6 Block 5-make 6

Block 6-make7 Block 7-make 6 Block 8-make7 Block 9-make 7 Block 10-make 7

Block 11-make 8 Block 12-make7 Block 13-make 7 Block 14-make 9 Block 15-make 7

Block 16-make 5 Block 17-make 7 Block 18-make 7 Block 19-make 7 Block 20-make 7

Block 21-make 7 Block 22-make 5 Block 23-make 7 Block 24-make 6 Block 25-make 7

LIGHT FABRICS

 GP70SF

 GP70DE

 GP70PH

 GP70OC

 GP70AL

 GP70SG

 *BM53TN

 BM53CD

 GP71LM

DARK FABRICS

 *GP70GN

 GP70TE

 GP70LN

 GP70SP

 BM53ON

 BM61RD

 GP01RD

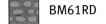 GP59CB

 GP59PU

 GP20PU

* Can be used as
light or dark
depending on fabric
used with it

70

Block 3	11	17	19	3	6	16	25	5	20	25	9	10
5	15	1	8	24	14	18	6	10	11	2	13	6
19	24	14	23	9	15	13	24	4	12	17	5	14
12	1	21	11	21	2	7	20	6	15	8	10	21
18	23	20	3	17	19	11	21	16	1	16	9	23
20	19	24	13	4	25	10	7	13	4	18	2	8
9	8	12	19	15	12	1	23	18	2	17	25	11
13	15	7	22	2	22	20	21	14	25	6	10	22
14	21	23	18	4	14	9	3	1	10	12	8	2
6	24	25	14	3	21	15	8	11	13	7	20	5
9	20	19	11	18	12	7	2	17	8	23	6	16
14	5	16	22	9	15	19	25	1	7	22	4	17
10	17	18	23	1	13	24	12	4	14	11	5	3

MAKING THE 9-PATCH BLOCKS

Use a ¼in (6mm) seam allowance throughout. Make 169 9-patch blocks, making each block as shown in the Block Assembly Diagram, positioning the darker fabric in the top left corner so that the checkerboard effect is consistent throughout the quilt. The quilt shown uses 25 different colour combinations as shown in the Block Colourways Diagram. Follow the Block Placement Diagram numbers for placement of each block.

MAKING THE QUILT

Take the 9-patch blocks and the plain squares and referring to the Block Placement Diagram and the Quilt Assembly Diagram lay out each diagonal row in turn. The Block Placement Diagram shows by block numbers where the blocks were placed in the quilt shown. If you prefer, you can create your own scrappy look by arranging your own block layout. The use of a design wall will help with placement.

Sew the blocks together into 25 diagonal rows, adding the setting triangles to the end of each row. Sew the rows together and then sew the corner triangles in place to complete the quilt centre.

Sew the shorter borders to the top and bottom of the quilt and then the longer borders to the sides of the quilt.

FINISHING THE QUILT

Press the quilt top. If using a standard-width backing, place the narrow strip between the wider backing pieces and join with a ¼in (6mm) seam allowance to form a piece approx. 105in x 105in (266.7cm x 266.7cm).

Layer the quilt top, batting and backing and baste together (see page 164).

Quilt as preferred. The quilt shown was quilted in the ditch around the pieced and the plain blocks and along the border seams.

Trim quilt edges and attach the binding (see page 165).

QUILT ASSEMBLY DIAGRAM

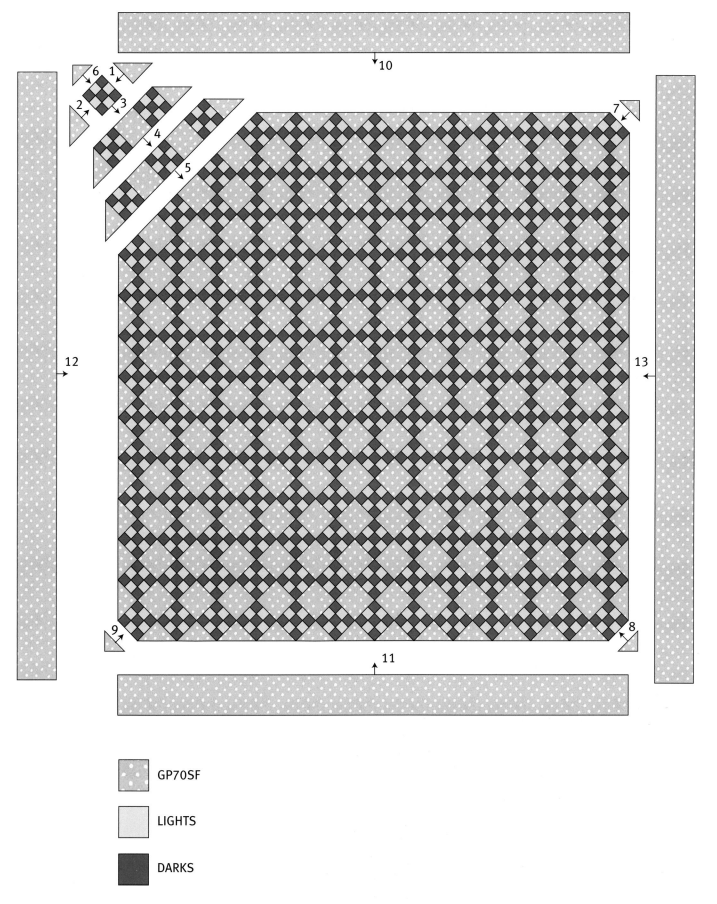

GP70SF

LIGHTS

DARKS

contrast columns **

Kaffe Fassett

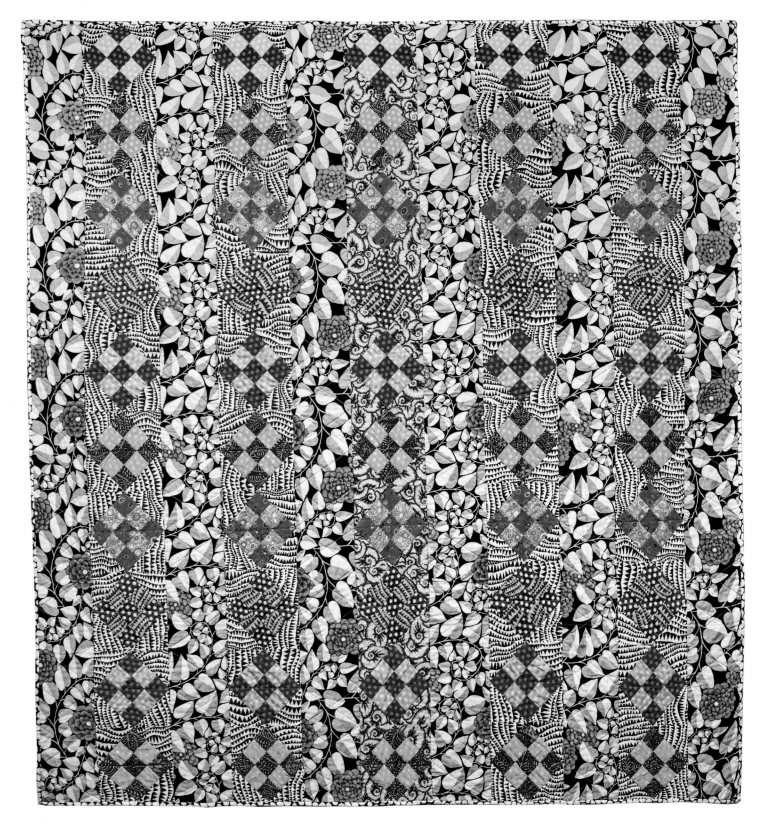

Simple 9-patch blocks have been used to great effect in this quilt, set on point within vertical columns of Vine fabric. The 9-patch blocks create bands running across the quilt, accentuated by using the same two fabrics for all the horizontally aligned blocks.

SIZE OF FINISHED QUILT
78½in x 85in (199.5cm x 216cm)

MATERIALS
Fabrics calculated at minimum width of 40in (101.6cm) and are cut across the width, unless otherwise stated

Patchwork Fabrics
VINE
Black	GP151BK	2½yd (2.3m)

SHARKS TEETH
Blue	BM60BL	2yd (1.8m)

CURLIQUE
Green	PJ87GN	½yd (45cm)

⅜yd (35cm) each of the following:
SPOT
Apple	GP70AL
Duck Egg	GP70DE
Charcoal	GP70CC
Sapphire	GP70SP

ROMAN GLASS
Emerald	GP01EM

FERNS
Purple	GP147PU

¼yd (25cm) each of the following:
SHARKS TEETH
Pink	BM60PK

ROMAN GLASS
Pink	GP01PK

Backing Fabric
BUTTON FLOWER
Contrast	GP152CO	6¼yd (5.75m)

Batting
86in x 93in (218.5cm x 236cm)

Binding
JUMBLE
White	BM53WH	¾yd (70cm)

Quilting Thread
Machine quilting thread

9-PATCH UNIT ASSEMBLY DIAGRAM

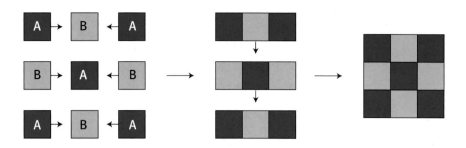

BLOCK ASSEMBLY DIAGRAM

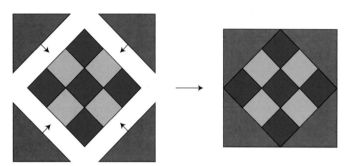

CUTTING OUT
Remove selvedges before cutting.
For the plain columns, from GP151BK, cut 6 strips *lengthwise,* each 6½in x 85½in (16.5cm x 217.2cm).
From BM60BL, cut 80 squares, each 5⅛in x 5⅛in (13cm x 13cm). Cut each square once on the diagonal to make 2 triangles from each square (160 triangles in total).
From PJ87GN, cut 20 squares each 5⅛in x 5⅛in (13cm x 13cm). Cut each square once on the diagonal to make 2 triangles from each square (40 triangles in total).
From all remaining fabric, cut squares, each 2½in x 2½in (6.4cm x 6.4cm), as follows:

GP70SP and GP147PU, cut 75 squares in each (A squares).
GP70CC and GP01EM, cut 50 squares in each (A squares).
GP70AL and GP70DE, cut 60 squares in each (B squares).
BM60PK and GP01PK, cut 40 squares in each (B squares).

Backing
From GP151BK, cut 2 lengths approx. 93in (236cm) long and 3 strips 8in x 32in (20.3cm x 81.3cm). Remove the selvedges.

Binding
From BM53WH, cut 9 strips 2½in (6.4cm) wide across the width. Remove selvedges and sew together end to end.

MAKING THE BLOCKS
Use a ¼in (6mm) seam allowance throughout.
Sew the squares into 9-patch units as shown in the 9-Patch Unit Assembly Diagram.
Make the following units in the combinations given below:
15 GP70SP + GP70DE; 15 GP147PU + GP70AL; 10 GP01EM + GP01PK; 10 GP70CC + BM60PK.

Sew each 9-patch unit into a larger block with a triangle on each side, as shown in the Block Assembly Diagram. Use BM60BL triangles where shown for 40 blocks and PJ87GN triangles for 10 blocks.

MAKING THE QUILT
Following the Quilt Assembly Diagram, sew the pieced blocks together into 5 columns of 10 blocks each, making sure every column has the same sequence of blocks from top to bottom. Make 4 BM60BL background columns. Make 1 PJ87GN background column.
Alternate the pieced columns with the plain GP151BK columns to make 11 columns in total. Sew the columns together.

FINISHING THE QUILT
Press the quilt top. Using a ¼in (6mm) seam allowance, sew the narrow backing pieces together end to end and then trim to 94in (238.8cm). Sew this narrow panel between the larger backing pieces to form a piece approx 87in x 94in (221cm x 238.8cm).
Layer the quilt top, batting and backing and baste together (see page 164). Quilt as preferred. The quilt shown was quilted in the ditch of all the blocks and the long panel seams. Lines were quilted vertically and horizontally through the centre of the 9-patch units. For the strippy panels, a zig zag quilting pattern was sewn vertically, from the point of a 9-patch unit to the centre point of the triangle on the opposite block. This was repeated in the opposite direction to create a diamond pattern.
Trim quilt edges and attach the binding (see page 165).

Tip
Most of the triangle patches have bias edges. The use of spray starch prior to cutting will help stabilize them until they are sewn. Take care when handling and pressing.

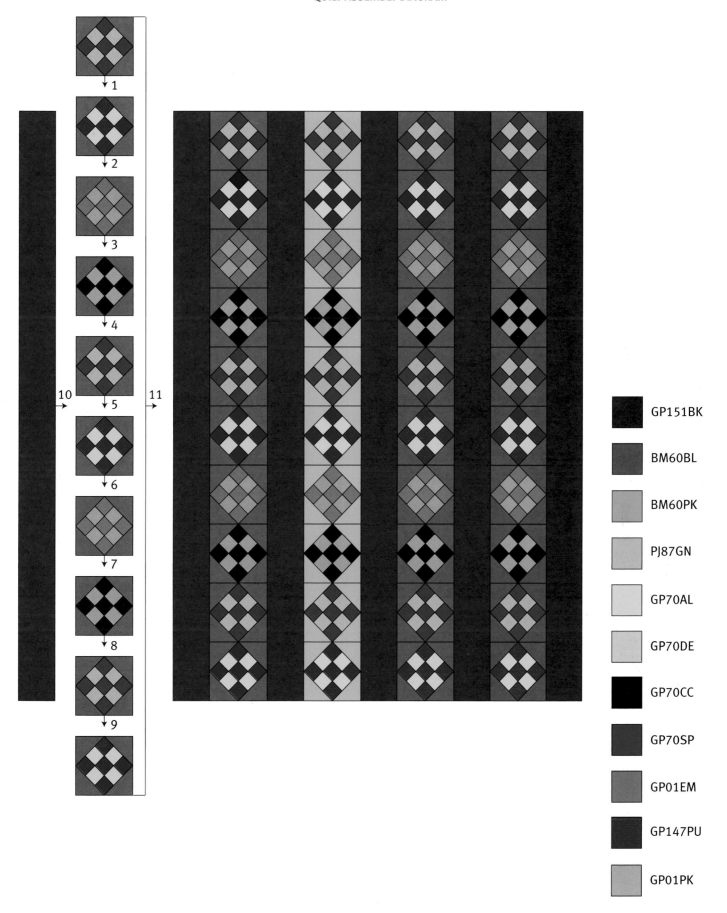

GP151BK

BM60BL

BM60PK

PJ87GN

GP70AL

GP70DE

GP70CC

GP70SP

GP01EM

GP147PU

GP01PK

coleus columns **

Liza Prior Lucy

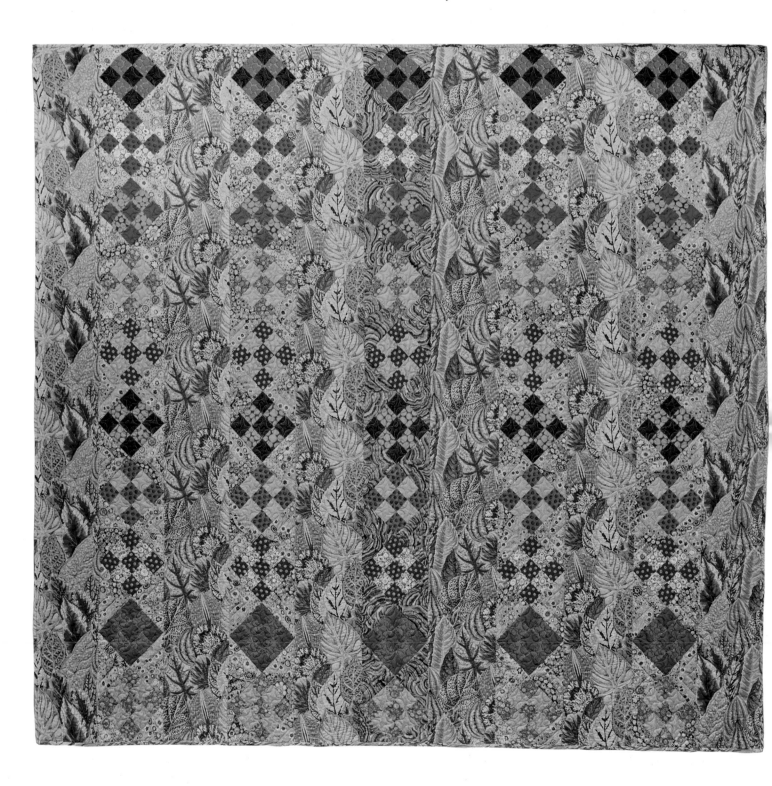

In selecting fabrics for my version of this quilt, I chose to stay close to the original American Museum quilt. The backgrounds of the 9-patch blocks and the columns merge except for the centre 9-patch background which is a departure from the rest. Philip Jacobs' new Coleus fabric sets the mood of this quilt.

SIZE OF FINISHED QUILT
93½in x 85in (237.5cm x 216cm)

MATERIALS
Fabrics calculated at minimum width of 40in (101.6cm) and are cut across the width, unless otherwise stated

Patchwork Fabrics
COLEUS
Moss   PJ30MS   5yd (4.6m)
(includes binding)
MILLEFIORE
Antique   GP92AN   2yd (1.8m)
TREE FUNGI
Teal   PJ82TE   ½yd (45cm)

⅜yd (35cm) each of the following:
SPOT
Plum   GP70PL
Peacock   GP70PC
ABORIGINAL DOT
Charcoal   GP71CC
Orchid   GP71OD
PAPERWEIGHT
Teal   GP20TE

¼yd (25cm) each of the following:
SPOT
Lichen   GP70LN
ABORIGINAL DOT
Leaf   GP71LF
JUMBLE
Maroon   BM53MR
Ochre   BM53OC
PAPERWEIGHT
Algae   GP20AL

Backing Fabric
Tree Fungi   PJ82TE   8yd (7.3m)

Binding
Use remaining PJ30MS

Batting
101in x 93in (256.5cm x 236cm)

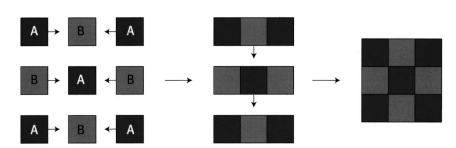

BLOCK ASSEMBLY DIAGRAM

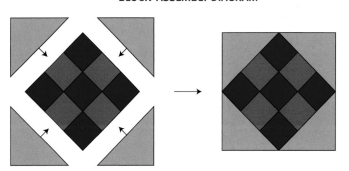

Quilting Thread
Machine quilting thread

CUTTING OUT
Remove all selvedges before cutting out.

For the plain columns, from PJ30MS, cut 6 strips *lengthwise*, each 9in x 85½in (23cm x 217.2cm). When cutting the columns, try to make each one different. From GP92AN, cut 80 squares, each 5⅛in x 5⅛in (13cm x 13cm). Cut each square once on the diagonal to make 2 triangles from each square (160 triangles in total). From PJ82TE, cut 20 squares each 5⅛in x 5⅛in (13cm x 13cm). Cut each square once on the diagonal to make 2 triangles from each square (40 triangles in total). From all remaining fabric, cut squares, each 2½in x 2½in (6.4cm x 6.4cm), as follows:
From GP70PL, GP70PC, GP71CC, GP71OD and GP20TE, cut 50 squares in each (A squares).
From GP70LN, GP71LF, BM53MR, BM53OC and GP20AL, cut 40 squares in each (B squares).

Backing
From PJ82TE cut 3 lengths approx. 93in (236.2cm) long. Remove the selvedges. Trim one of the lengths to a width of 23in (58.4cm).

Binding
From the remaining PJ30MS, cut 5 strips *lengthwise*, each 2½in x 85½in (6.4cm x 217.2cm). Sew end to end.

MAKING THE BLOCKS
Use a ¼in (6mm) seam allowance throughout.
Sew the squares into 9-patch units as shown in the 9-Patch Unit Assembly Diagram. Make 5 of each combination as follows: GP71OD and BM53MR; GP70PC and GP20AL; GP71CC and BM53OC; GP20TE and GP71LF; GP70PL and GP70LN; GP71OD and BM53OC; GP70PC and GP71LF; GP70PL and GP20AL; GP71CC and BM53MR; GP20TE and GP70LN.
Sew each 9-patch unit into a larger block with a triangle on each side, as in the Block Assembly Diagram (above). Use GP92AN triangles where shown on the Quilt Assembly Diagram for 40 blocks and PJ82TE triangles for 10 blocks.

MAKING THE QUILT

Following the Quilt Assembly Diagram, sew the pieced blocks together into 5 columns of 10 blocks each, making sure every column has the same sequence of blocks from top to bottom. Make 4 GP92AN background columns and 1 PJ82TE background column.

Making sure the leaves of the PJ30MS strips are all upright, alternate the pieced columns with the plain columns to make 11 columns in total. Sew the columns together.

FINISHING THE QUILT

Press the quilt top. Sew the backing pieces together using a ¼in (6mm) seam allowance. Sew the narrow panel between the two wide panels to form a piece approx. 101in x 93in (256.5cm x 236.2cm).

Layer the quilt top, batting and backing and baste together (see page 164). Quilt as preferred. The quilt shown was quilted in the ditch around the sashing and strips. Concave diamond shapes were quilted in alternate small squares of each 9-patch. Free-motion quilting of leaves followed the flowing patterns of the Coleus fabric design.

Trim the quilt edges and attach the binding (see page 165).

PJ30MS	GP71CC
GP92AN	GP71OD
PJ82TE	GP71LF
GP7OPL	GP20TE
GP70PC	GP20AL
GP70LN	BM53MR
	BM53OC

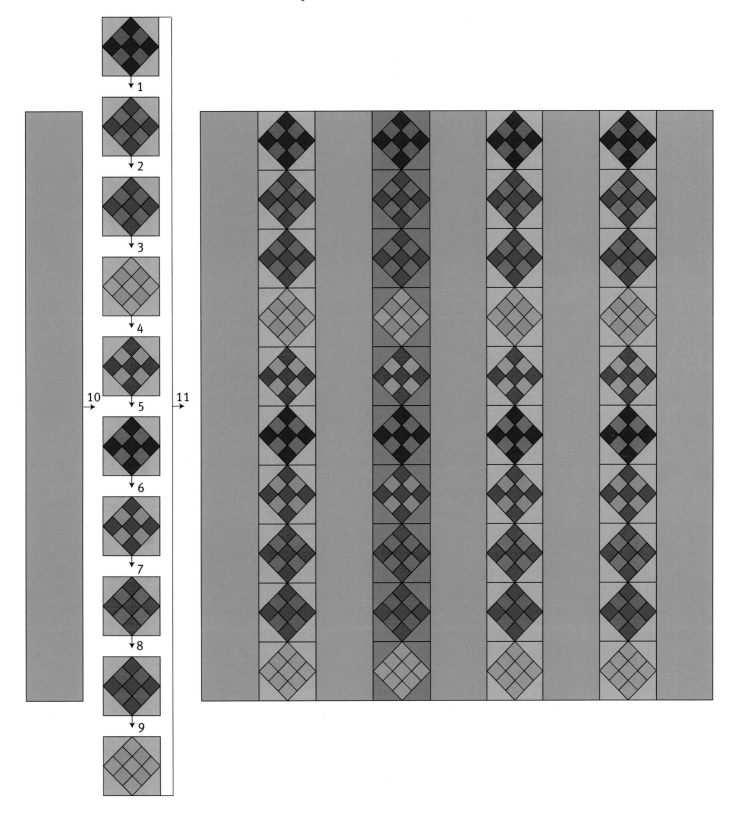

autumn **

Kaffe Fassett

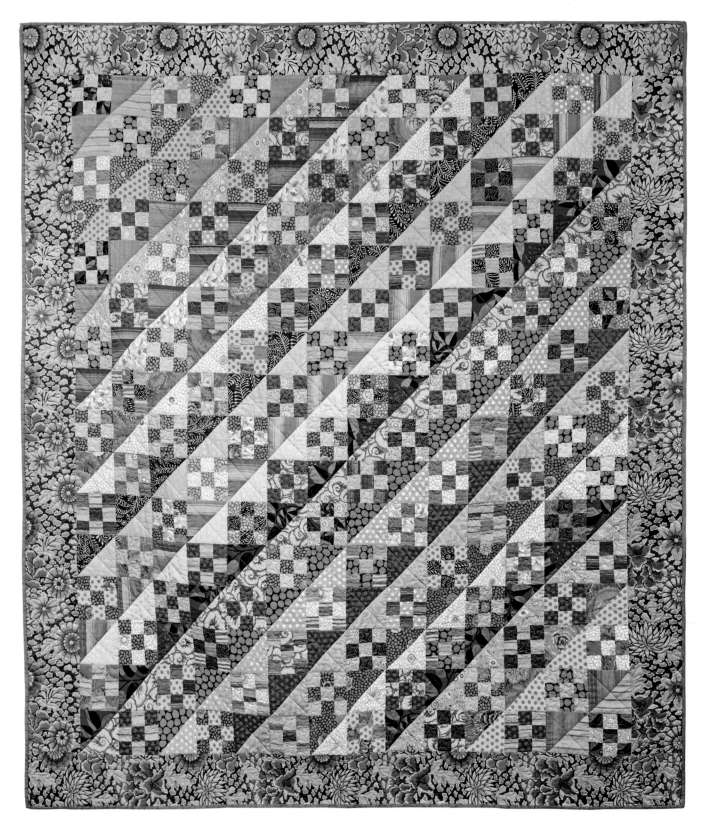

This quilt has diagonal rows of deliberately placed triangles alternating with scrappy 9-patch blocks. The 9-patch blocks are in two different light/dark arrangements. It is not necessary to make and place each 9-patch as in the quilt shown, but it is important to place the triangles exactly, so as to create the strong diagonals.

SIZE OF FINISHED QUILT
75in x 84in (190.5cm x 213.4cm)

MATERIALS
Fabrics calculated at minimum width of 40in (101.6cm) and are cut across the width, unless otherwise stated

Patchwork and Border Fabrics
DREAM
Brown   GP148BR   2¼yd (2m)

½yd (45cm) each of the following:
SPOT
Cocoa   GP70CC
GUINEA FLOWER
Gold   GP59GD
Brown   GP59BR
ROMAN GLASS
Gold   GP01GD
VINE
Royal   GP151RY

⅜yd (35cm) each of the following:
ABORIGINAL DOT
Ochre   GP71OC
SPOT
Peach   GP70PH
Gold   GP70GD
JUMBLE
Animal   BM53AM
BRASSICA
Rust   PJ51RU
CURLIQUE
Ochre   PJ87OC
WOVEN EXOTIC STRIPE
Dusk   WESDU
Warm   WESWM

¼yd (25cm) each of the following:
WOVEN EXOTIC STRIPE
Earth   WESER
WOVEN CATERPILLAR STRIPE
Yellow   WCSYE
ABORIGINAL DOT
Chocolate   GP71CL

FERNS
Black   GP147BL
GUINEA FLOWER
Apricot   GP59AP
SPOT
Yellow   GP70YE
Sherbet   GP70SB
WOVEN ALTERNATING STRIPE
Yellow   WASYE
BAUBLES
Yellow   BM61YE

Backing Fabric
ROMAN GLASS
Byzantine   GP01BY   5½yd (5m)

Binding
ABORIGINAL DOT
Pumpkin   GP71PN   ¾yd (70cm)

Batting
83in x 92in (211cm x 234cm)

Quilting Thread
Machine quilting thread

CUTTING OUT
Remove all selvedges before cutting out fabric.

Border
From GP148BR and cutting along the *length* of the fabric, cut 2 lengths 6½in x 75½in (16.5cm x 192cm) for the top and bottom borders, and 2 lengths 6½in x 72½in (16.5cm x 184.2cm) for the side borders.

Half-square Triangle Blocks
These blocks are made by cutting squares 5⅜in x 5⅜in (13.7cm x 13.7cm) and then cutting each square once diagonally to make 2 triangles from each square. Cut these patches first, as they need to be cut in specific quantities for placement in diagonal "rows" of the quilt. Follow the list below to cut the numbers of squares given. Cut each square in half once diagonally to make 2 triangles:
GP70CC: 5 squares (10 triangles);
GP59GD: 9 squares (18 triangles);
GP59BR: 6 squares (12 triangles);
GP01GD: 6 squares (12 triangles);
GP151RY: 10 squares (20 triangles);
GP71OC: 5 squares (10 triangles);
GP70PH: 6 squares (12 triangles);
GP70GD: 4 squares (8 triangles);
BM53AM: 6 squares (12 triangles);
PJ51RU: 7 squares (14 triangles);
PJ87OC: 7 squares (14 triangles);
WESDU: 7 squares (14 triangles);
WESWM: 4 squares (8 triangles);
WESER: 5 squares (10 triangles);
GP147BL: 6 squares (12 triangles);
GP70YE: 7 squares (14 triangles);
GP70SB: 6 squares (12 triangles);
WASYE: 2 squares (4 triangles) and
BM61YE: 4 squares (8 triangles).

9-Patch Blocks

Cut all the remaining patchwork fabric into 2in (5cm) squares for the scrappy 9-patch blocks. There is no need to make each block exactly as in this quilt. Cut in sets of 4 of one colour and sets of 5 of a second colour to make each block. Note that there are two arrangements of 9-patch blocks. Block A has five dark squares and four light. Block B has five light squares and four dark. You will need to make 112 blocks in total. The quilt shown has 59 of Block A and 53 of Block B.

Backing

From GP01BY cut 2 lengths each approx. 83in (211cm) long. Remove the selvedges. From the remaining fabric cut 3 rectangles each 13in (33cm) wide x 28in (71.1cm) long.

Binding

From GP71PU cut 9 strips 2½in (6.4cm) wide across the width. Remove the selvedges and sew together end to end.

MAKING THE BLOCKS

Use a ¼in (6mm) seam allowance throughout.

Half-square Triangle Blocks

Follow the Half-Square Triangle Block Assembly Diagram to make triangle blocks out of two different coloured triangles. To create the effect of diagonal "rows", where Row 1 is at the top left and Row 14 at the bottom right, make triangle blocks as listed below (for a total of 112 blocks).

4 blocks WESER + WASYE; 4 blocks GP59BR + GP70GD; 6 blocks WESER + GP01GD; 8 blocks WESWM + BM61YE; 10 blocks PJ51RU +GP59GD; 12 blocks GP147BL + GP70PH; 14 blocks WESDU + GP70YE; 14 blocks GP151RY + PJ87OC; 12 blocks BM53AM + GP70SB; 10 blocks GP70CC + GP71OC; 8 blocks GP59BR + GP59GD; 6 blocks GP151RY + GP01GD; 4 blocks PJ51RU + GP70GD.

9-Patch Blocks

Follow the 9-Patch Blocks Assembly Diagram to make 9-patch blocks using 4 squares of one colour and 5 of another. (Note the different arrangement of lights and darks in Block A and Block B.)

MAKING THE QUILT

Following the Quilt Assembly Diagram carefully, lay out all the blocks into 16 rows of 14 blocks each. Alternate the 9-patch and triangle blocks. Place the triangle blocks so that they form diagonal "rows". Each diagonal row comprises identical triangle blocks, with each block positioned with its diagonal seam running from bottom left to top right with the dark fabric above the seam. The arrangement of A and B 9-patch blocks can be as you choose or you can follow the diagram.

Sew the blocks into rows. Sew the rows together.

HALF-SQUARE TRIANGLE BLOCK ASSEMBLY DIAGRAM

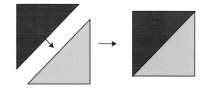

9- PATCH BLOCKS ASSEMBLY DIAGRAM

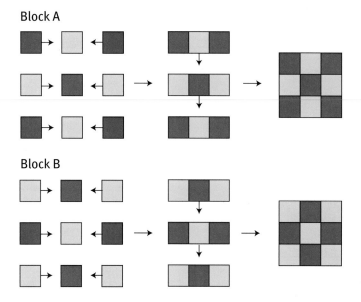

Triangles and 9-patch blocks

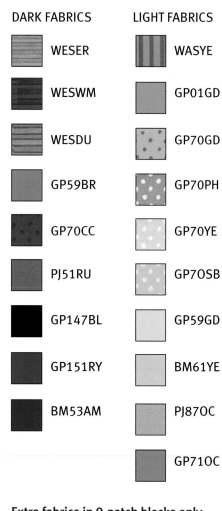

DARK FABRICS	LIGHT FABRICS
WESER	WASYE
WESWM	GP01GD
WESDU	GP70GD
GP59BR	GP70PH
GP70CC	GP70YE
PJ51RU	GP70SB
GP147BL	GP59GD
GP151RY	BM61YE
BM53AM	PJ87OC
	GP71OC

Extra fabrics in 9-patch blocks only

GP71CL

GP59AP WCSYE

Border fabric

GP148BR

84

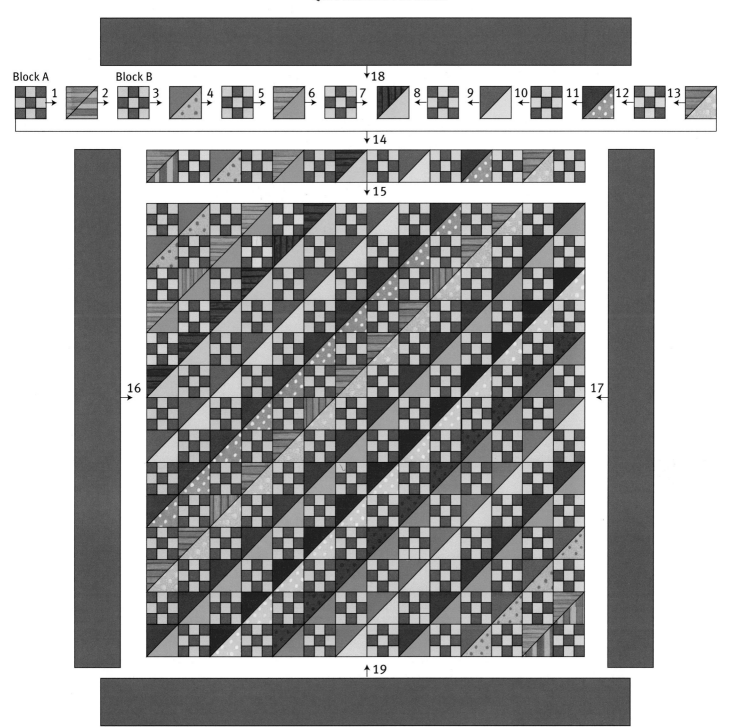

Border

As GP148BR is directional, each border strip was cut down the length of the fabric, to create the effect of the pattern running around the quilt centre.
Sew the shorter border lengths to each side of the quilt centre and then sew the longer border lengths to the top and bottom.

FINISHING THE QUILT

Press the quilt top. Using a ¼in (6mm) seam allowance, sew the 13in x 28in (33cm x 71.1cm) rectangles of backing fabric together end to end to make a strip approx. 13in x 83in (33cm x 211cm). Sew this strip between the wider backing pieces to make a backing approx. 83in x 92in (211cm x 234cm).

Layer the quilt top, batting and backing and baste together (see page 164). Quilt as preferred. The quilt shown was quilted in the ditch around all squares and diamonds. Within the 9-patch squares there are in-fills of curvy, concave diamond shapes.
Trim the quilt edges and attach the binding (see page 165).

moonlight ✳✳

Kaffe Fassett

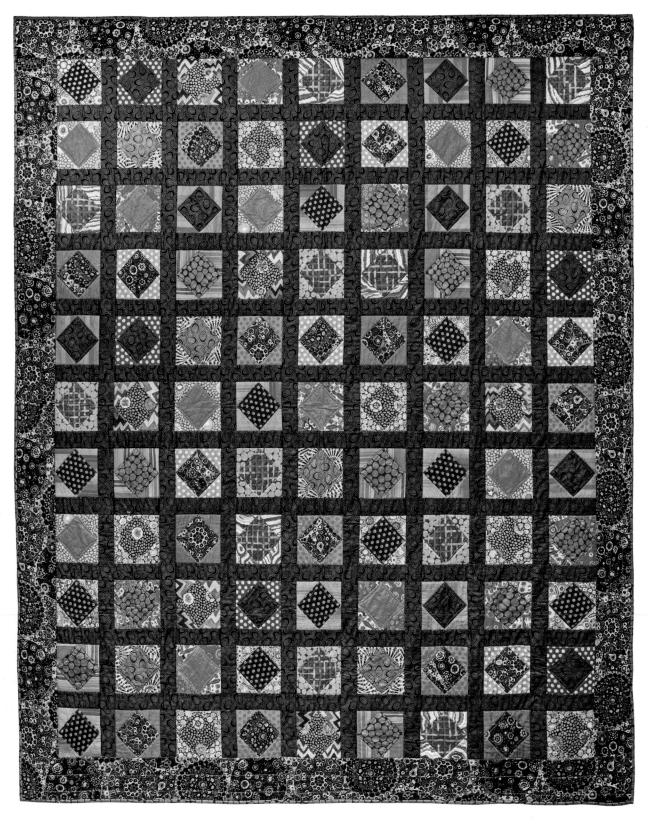

The original inspiration for this quilt was made in luxurious satins and silks. For this version, cottons in rich purples and blues (cool colours) and reds and pinks (hot colours) have been used. The on-point square-in-a-square blocks are separated by dark sashing, helping to showcase the fabrics, while a wide border frames the design.

SIZE OF FINISHED QUILT
75½in x 90½in (191.8cm x 230cm)

MATERIALS
Fabrics calculated at minimum width of 40in (101.6cm) and are cut across the width, unless otherwise stated

Patchwork and Border Fabrics
ABORIGINAL DOT
Orchid   GP71OD   2⅝yd (2.4m)

MILLEFIORE
Dark   GP92DK   2⅜yd (2.2m)
Red   GP92RD   ⅜yd (35cm)

⅜yd (35cm) each of the following:
JUMBLE
Blue   BM53BL
GUINEA FLOWER
Purple   GP59PU
SPOT
Black   GP70BK
MAD PLAID
Charcoal   BM37CC
ABORIGINAL DOT
Charcoal   GP71CC

¼yd (25cm) each of the following:
PAPERWEIGHT
Jewel   GP20JL
JUMBLE
Ochre   BM53OC
MILLEFIORE
Blue   GP92BL
GUINEA FLOWER
Brown   GP59BR
JUPITER
Blue   GP131BL
PAPER FANS
Black   GP143BK
SPOT
Tobacco   GP70TO
Sapphire   GP70SP
Royal   GP70RY

ABORIGINAL DOT
Plum   GP71PL
Chocolate   GP71CL
WOVEN BROAD STRIPE
Blue   WBSBL
WOVEN EXOTIC STRIPE
Parma   WESPA
Mallard   WESML
SOUND WAVES
Green   BM62GN

Backing Fabric
DREAM
Dark   GP148DK   6⅝yd (6m)

Batting
84in x 99in (213.4cm x 251.5cm)

Binding
JUMBLE
Blue   BM53BL   ¾yd (70cm)

Quilting Thread
Machine quilting thread

PATCHES
The blocks are made up of 4⅜in (11.1cm) centre squares, with 3⅝in (9.2cm) triangles in each corner. The sashing is 2½in (6.4cm) wide and the border is 5½in (14cm) wide. There are 16 different block colourways in the quilt. The colours of the background triangles in each block alternate between 'cool' and 'hot' shades.

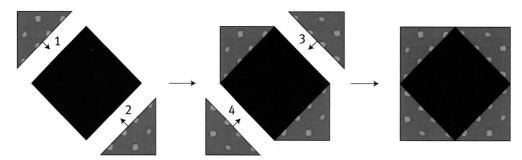

CUTTING OUT

Remove all selvedges before cutting out. Note that the fabrics used for the sashing strips and the border are cut from the *length* of the fabric to avoid joins.

Sashing Strips

From GP71OD, cut 10 strips down the length of the fabric, each 2½in x 66in (6.4cm x 167.6cm) long for horizontal sashing strips.
Cut 88 rectangles each 2½in x 6in (6.4cm x 15.2cm) for vertical sashing strips.
Keep the remaining fabric for cutting 4⅜in (11.1cm) block central squares.

Border Strips

From GP92DK, cutting down the *length* of the fabric, cut 2 strips 5½in x 81in (14cm x 205.7cm) and 2 strips 5½in x 76in (14cm x 193cm). Keep the remaining fabric for cutting the block central squares.

Block Central Squares

Cut the following number of 4⅜in x 4⅜in (11.1cm x 11.1cm) squares (for a total of 99).
12 in GP71OD; 18 in GP92DK; 13 in BM53BL; 13 in GP59PU; 13 in GP70BK; 12 in BM37CC; 12 in GP71CC and 6 in GP71CL.

Block Triangles

Cut the following number of 3⅝in x 3⅝in (9.2cm x 9.2cm) squares and cut each once on the diagonal to give 2 triangles (for a total of 198 squares/396 triangles):
24 squares in GP92RD (48 triangles);
14 squares in GP20JL (28 triangles);
12 squares in BM53OC (24 triangles);
14 squares in GP92BL (28 triangles);
12 squares in GP59BR (24 triangles);
12 squares in GP131BL (24 triangles);
12 squares in GP143BK (24 triangles);
12 squares in GP70TO (24 triangles);
12 squares in GP70SP (24 triangles);
12 squares in GP70RY (24 triangles);
12 squares in GP71PL (24 triangles);
12 squares in WBSBL (24 triangles);
14 squares in WESPA (28 triangles);
12 squares in WESML (24 triangles) and
12 squares in BM62GN (24 triangles).

Backing

From GP148DK, cut 2 lengths approx. 100in (254cm) long. From the remaining fabric, cut 3 rectangles 6in x 34in (15.2cm x 86.4cm). Remove the selvedges.

Binding

From BM53BL, cut 10 strips 2½in (6.4cm) across the width. Remove the selvedges and sew together end to end.

MAKING THE QUILT
Square-in-a-Square Blocks

Use a ¼in (6mm) seam allowance throughout.
For each block, sew the triangles to the on-point square as shown in the Block Assembly Diagram. Make blocks in the following combinations of 1 square and 4 identical triangles.
6 blocks in GP71OD and GP70RY; 6 blocks in GP71OD and WBSBL; 6 blocks in GP92DK and GP70TO; 6 blocks in GP92DK and GP70SP; 6 blocks in GP92DK and GP71PL; 6 blocks in BM53BL and GP92RD; 7 blocks in BM53BL and WESPA; 7 blocks in GP59PU and GP20JL; 6 blocks in GP59PU and BM62BL; 7 blocks in GP70BK and GP92BL; 6 blocks in GP70BK and WESML; 6 blocks in BM37CC and BM53OC; 6 blocks in BM37CC and GP131BL; 6 blocks in GP71CC and GP92RD; 6 blocks in GP71CC and GP59BR and 6 blocks in GP71CL and GP143BK.

ASSEMBLING THE QUILT

Lay the blocks out in 11 rows of 9 blocks each, as shown in the Quilt Assembly Diagram, alternating those with cool colour triangles with those with hot colours. (Or choose your own order, using a design wall to help with placing.)
Sew the blocks in each row together with a GP71OD vertical sashing strip between each block. Then sew the rows together, with a GP71OD horizontal sashing strip between each row. To make sure the horizontal sashing strips fit, crease or mark the centre of the strip and also mark the centre of the block row and then pin together at these marks. Pin together at the beginning and end of the row, adding further pins and easing to fit as needed. Add the borders, sewing the long GP92DK border strips to the sides of the quilt and the shorter GP92DK border strips to the top and bottom.

FINISHING THE QUILT

Press the quilt top. Using a ¼in (6mm) seam allowance, sew the 6in x 34in (15.2cm x 86.4cm) backing rectangles end to end. Sew this narrow panel between the larger pieces to form a piece approx. 85in x 100in (216cm x 254cm). Layer the quilt top, batting and backing and baste together (see page 164). Quilt as preferred. The quilt shown was quilted in the ditch around the large squares and borders. A small arc was quilted from each of the corners of the on-point squares. Two parallel lines were quilted in the vertical and horizontal borders.
Trim the quilt edges and attach the binding (see page 165).

QUILT ASSEMBLY DIAGRAM

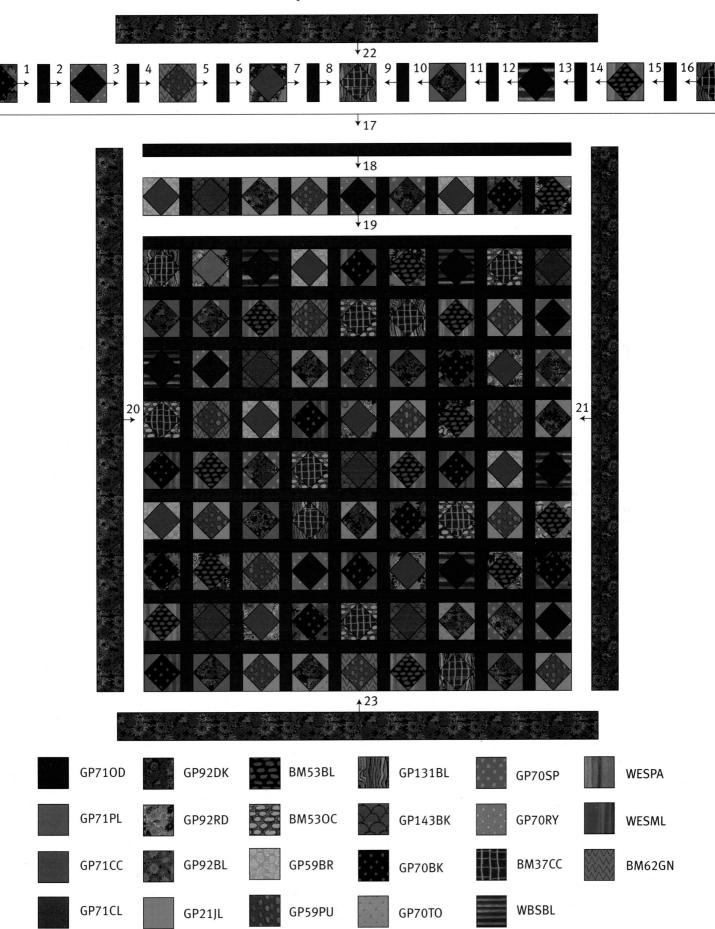

GP71OD

GP71PL

GP71CC

GP71CL

GP92DK

GP92RD

GP92BL

GP21JL

BM53BL

BM53OC

GP59BR

GP59PU

GP131BL

GP143BK

GP70BK

GP70TO

GP70SP

GP70RY

BM37CC

WESPA

WESML

BM62GN

WBSBL

sashed baskets ***

Kaffe Fassett

Colourful flower basket blocks are arranged in an on-point setting for this quilt, framed by bold sashing. A simple border using the same fabric as the sashing surrounds the design.

SIZE OF FINISHED QUILT
79in x 79in (201cm x 201cm)

MATERIALS
Fabrics calculated at minimum width of 40in (101.6cm) and are cut across the width, unless otherwise stated

Patchwork and Border Fabrics
PAINTED POTS
Red	PWKF02RD	$\frac{3}{8}$yd (35cm)
Orange	PWKF02OR	$\frac{3}{8}$yd (35cm)
Pink	PWKF02PK	$\frac{3}{8}$yd (35cm)
Yellow	PWKF02YE	$\frac{3}{8}$yd (35cm)

SPOT
White	GP70WH	$2\frac{1}{2}$yd (2.3m)

GERBERA
Blue	PWKF06BL	$\frac{7}{8}$yd (80cm)

SHARKS TEETH
Blue	BM60BL	$3\frac{1}{2}$yd (3.2m)

Backing Fabric
LAKE BLOSSOM
Sky	GP93SK	$6\frac{1}{4}$yd (5.7m)

Binding
JUMBLE
White	BM53WH	$\frac{3}{4}$yd (70cm)

Batting
88in x 88in (223.5cm x 223.5cm)

Quilting Thread
Machine quilting thread

PATCHES
The basket blocks are made up of the following shapes.
Triangle A: $6\frac{7}{8}$in (17.5cm).
Triangle B: $2\frac{7}{8}$in (7.3cm).
Rectangle C: $2\frac{1}{2}$in x $6\frac{1}{2}$in (6.4cm x 16.5cm).
Triangle D: $2\frac{3}{4}$in (7cm).
Triangle E: $4\frac{7}{8}$in (12.4cm).

CUTTING OUT
Remove selvedges from all fabrics before cutting. All patches can be cut from strips, cut across the width of the fabric. Patches include a seam allowance of $\frac{1}{4}$in (6mm).
Note: The triangles will have bias edges. Use spray starch prior to cutting to help stabilize them until they are sewn. Take care when handling and pressing.

Basket Blocks
There are 25 Basket blocks in the quilt. See the Block Assembly Diagram (overleaf) to identify the A, B, C, D and E patch shapes used in the blocks.

Triangle A: Cut strips $6\frac{7}{8}$in (17.5cm) across the fabric width. Cut into $6\frac{7}{8}$in x $6\frac{7}{8}$in (17.5cm x 17.5cm) squares. Cut each square once diagonally to make 2 triangles. Each strip will give 5 squares (10 triangles).
Cut 13 squares (25 triangles) in PWKF06BL, 4 squares (7 triangles) in PWKF02YE, 3 squares (6 triangles) in PWKF02RD, PWKF02OR and PWKF02PK.

Triangle B: Cut strips $2\frac{7}{8}$in (7.3cm) across the fabric width. Cut the strips into $2\frac{7}{8}$in x $2\frac{7}{8}$in (7.3cm x 7.3cm) squares. Cut each square once diagonally to make 2 triangles. Each strip will give 13 squares (26 triangles).
Cut 88 squares (175 triangles) in GP70WH, 25 squares (49 triangles) in PWKF02YE, 21 squares (42 triangles) each in PWKF02RD, PWKF02OR and PWKF02PK.

Rectangle C: In GP70WH cut $2\frac{1}{2}$in (6.4cm) strips across the fabric width. Cut rectangles $6\frac{1}{2}$in x $2\frac{1}{2}$in (16.5cm x 6.4cm). Each strip will give 6 rectangles. Cut 50 in total.

Triangle D: In PWKF06BL cut strips $2\frac{3}{4}$in (7cm) across the fabric width. Cut the strips into $2\frac{3}{4}$in x $2\frac{3}{4}$in (7cm x 7cm) squares. Cut each square once diagonally to make 2 triangles. Each strip will give 14 squares (28 triangles). Cut 25 squares (50 triangles) in total.

Triangle E: In GP70WH cut strips $4\frac{7}{8}$in (12.4cm) across the fabric width. Cut the strips into $4\frac{7}{8}$in x $4\frac{7}{8}$in (12.4cm x 12.4cm) squares. Cut each square once diagonally to make 2 triangles. Each strip will give 8 squares (16 triangles). Cut 13 squares (25 triangles) in total.

Sashing
In BM60BL cut $3\frac{1}{2}$in (9cm) strips across the fabric width. Cut rectangles $3\frac{1}{2}$in x $10\frac{1}{2}$in (9cm x 26.7cm). Each strip will give 3 rectangles per strip. Cut 64 in total.

Sashing Corner Posts
In BM60BL cut 24 squares $3\frac{1}{2}$in x $3\frac{1}{2}$in (9cm x 9cm) from the fabric remaining from cutting the sashing rectangles.

Sashing End Triangles
In BM60BL, use leftover fabric to cut 4 squares $5\frac{3}{8}$in x $5\frac{3}{8}$in (13.6cm x 13.6cm). On each square cut along both diagonals to make 4 triangles, for 16 triangles in total.

Setting Triangles
In GP70WH, cut 3 squares $15\frac{3}{8}$in x $15\frac{3}{8}$in (39cm x 39cm) – you will need 2 strips $15\frac{3}{8}$in (39cm) x width of fabric. Cut each of the squares along both diagonals to make 4 triangles (for a total of 12 triangles).

Corner Triangles
In GP70WH cut 2 squares $7\frac{7}{8}$in x $7\frac{7}{8}$in (20cm x 20cm). Cut each square once diagonally to make 4 triangles.

Border
In BM60BL, cut 8 strips $3\frac{1}{2}$in (9cm) x width of fabric. Sew the strips together end to end. Cut two lengths $3\frac{1}{2}$in x 74in (9cm x 188cm) for the sides of the quilt. Cut two lengths $3\frac{1}{2}$in x 80in (9cm x 203.2cm) for the top and bottom.

Backing
In GP93SK, cut 2 pieces 40in (102cm) x 88in (223.5cm) and 2 pieces 9in x $44\frac{1}{2}$in (23cm x 113cm). Sew the 2 narrow pieces together end to end, for an approximate length of 88in (223.5cm).

Binding
In BM53WH, cut 9 strips $2\frac{1}{2}$in (6.4cm) x width of fabric. Sew the strips together end to end.

BLOCK ASSEMBLY DIAGRAM

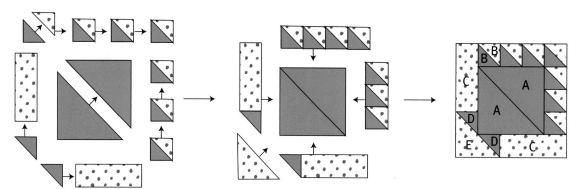

MAKING THE BLOCKS

Use a ¼in (6mm) seam allowance throughout. The 25 blocks all use the same Spot white (GP70WH) and Gerbera blue fabrics (PWKF06BL) but four different Painted Pots fabric colours (red, orange, pink and yellow).

Make 6 blocks each using red PWKF02RD, orange PWKF02OR, pink PWKF02PK and 7 blocks using yellow PWKF02YE.

Assemble each block as follows (see Block Assembly Diagram). Sew two Triangle A patches together. Sew two Triangle B patches together and repeat to make 7 half-square triangle (HST) units. Sew 4 HST units together and 3 HSTs together, as shown. Sew a Triangle D patch to the end of a Rectangle C patch and repeat once more. Sew the units together as shown, finishing with a Triangle E patch in the bottom left corner.

MAKING THE QUILT

Referring to the Quilt Assembly Diagram, lay out the blocks, sashing strips, corner posts and sashing triangles in diagonal rows. Sew the diagonal rows together, ending each sashing row with a sashing triangle, and ending each block row with a setting triangle. Sew all the rows together. Add a corner triangle to each corner to complete the quilt centre. Sew the shorter border strips to the sides of the quilt and the longer strips to the top and bottom.

FINISHING THE QUILT

Press the quilt top. Remove the selvedges from the backing pieces, place the narrow strip between the wider backing pieces and join with a ¼in (6mm) seam

allowance to form a piece approx. 88in x 88in (223.5cm x 223.5cm).

Layer the quilt top, batting and backing and baste together (see page 164).

Quilt as preferred. The quilt shown was quilted in the ditch around the border, triangles and blocks. A circle and spiral pattern was quilted in the centre of the blocks. Curved lines were quilted following the fabric pattern in the sashing and borders. Trim quilt edges and attach the binding (see page 165).

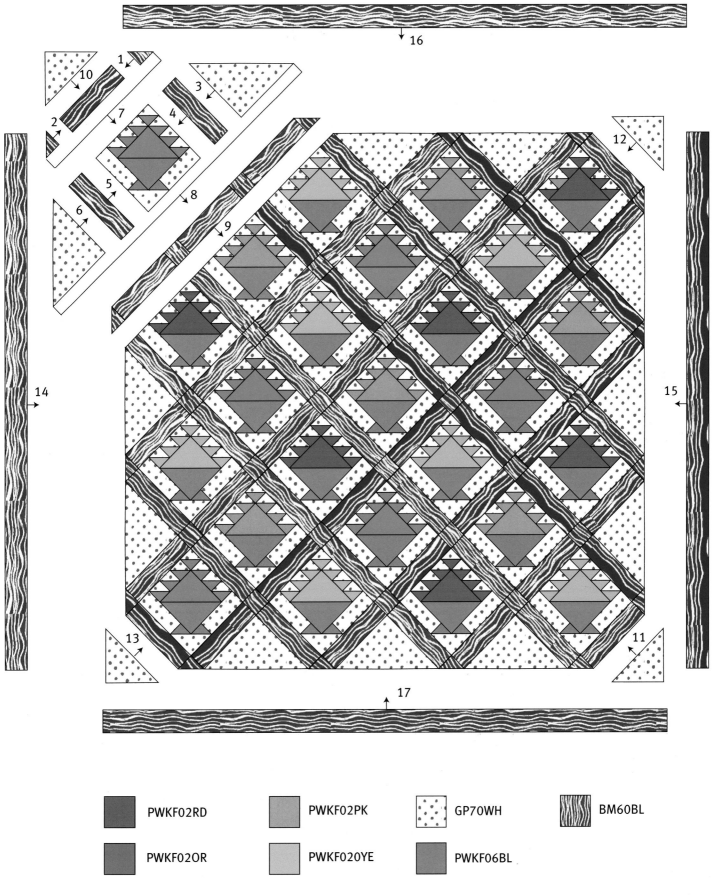

	PWKF02RD		PWKF02PK		GP70WH		BM60BL
	PWKF02OR		PWKF02OYE		PWKF06BL		

pastel 9-patch *

Kaffe Fassett

This is a scrappy quilt, so it is not necessary to place each fabric as in the original, but we have divided the fabrics into three groups, to make it easier to work out how to create the same effect with your own choices of fabrics.

SIZE OF FINISHED QUILT
72in x 80in (183cm x 203cm)

MATERIALS
Fabrics calculated at minimum width of 40in (101.6cm) and are cut across the width, unless otherwise stated

Patchwork Fabrics
GLORY		
*Pastel	PJ85PT	½yd (45cm)
SUMMER BOUQUET		
*Grey	PJ86GY	½yd (45cm)
BRASSICA		
*Pastel	PJ51PT	½yd (45cm)
HORSE CHESTNUT		
*Yellow	PJ84YE	½yd (45cm)
SHELL BOUQUET		
*Pastel	PJ88PT	½yd (45cm
LAKE BLOSSOM		
*Pink	GP93PK	½yd (45cm)
ABORIGINAL DOT		
**Mint	GP71MT	½yd (45cm)
MILLEFIORE		
***Pastel	GP92PT	½yd (45cm)
***Pink	GP92PK	⅝yd (60cm)
ROMAN GLASS		
**Pastel	GP01PT	¼yd (25cm)
GUINEA FLOWER		
**Grey	GP59GY	¼yd (25cm)
**Mauve	GP59MV	½yd (45cm)
***Turquoise	GP59TQ	½yd (45cm)
SPOT		
**Mint	GP70MT	¼yd (25cm)
**Hydrangea	GP70HY	½yd (45cm)
**Sky	GP70SK	½yd (45cm)
**Soft blue	GP70SF	½yd (45cm)
SHARKS TEETH		
***Red	BM60RD	½yd (45cm)
**Pink	BM60PK	½yd (45cm)
MAD PLAID		
**Pastel	BM37PT	½yd (45cm)
ZIG ZAG		
**Pink	BM43PK	½yd (45cm)]
JUMBLE		
**Candy	BM53CD	½yd (45cm)

Backing Fabric
MAPLE STREAM		
Ice	PJ80IC	5yd (4.6m)

Binding
ABORIGINAL DOT		
Mint	GP71MT	¾yd (70cm)

Batting
80in x 88in (203cm x 223.5cm)

Quilting Thread
Machine quilting thread

CUTTING OUT
Remove selvedges before cutting fabric.

There are three sizes of square and one size of rectangle in this quilt.
Cut each large square 8½in x 8½in (21.6cm x 21.6cm).
Cut each medium square 4½in x 4½in (11.4cm x 11.4cm).
Cut each small square 2½in x 2½in (6.4cm x 6.4cm).
Cut each rectangle 2½in x 4½in (6.4cm x 11.4cm).

Group 1 Fabrics (*)
These 6 fabrics are used only for the large squares: PJ85PT, PJ86GY, PJ51PT, PJ84YE, PJ88PT, GP93PK.

Group 2 Fabrics (**)
These 12 fabrics are used only in the medium and small squares, and the rectangles: GP71MT, GP01PT, GP59GY, GP59MV, GP70MT, GP70HY, GP70SK, GP70SF, BM60PK, BM37PT, BM43PK, BM53CD.

Group 3 Fabrics (***)
These 4 fabrics are used for all sizes: GP92PT, GP92PK, GP59TQ, BM60RD.

Large Squares
Cut between 2 and 8 squares each from Group 1 and Group 3 fabrics to make a total of 45 squares (plain blocks).

Medium and Small Squares, and Rectangles
The Group 2 fabrics and the remaining Group 3 fabrics are cut to be sewn into pieced blocks. For each block, choose two fabrics. Cut one fabric into 1 medium square and 4 matching small squares. Cut the other fabric into 4 rectangles. Cut sets to make a total of 45 blocks.

Backing
Cut 2 lengths approximately 88in (223.5cm) long. Remove the selvedges.

Binding
From GP71MT cut 9 strips 2½in (6.4cm) wide across the width of the fabric. Remove selvedges and sew end to end.

MAKING THE BLOCKS
Use a ¼in (6mm) seam allowance throughout.
Follow the Block Assembly Diagram to sew the pieced 9-patch blocks. Sew 45 blocks in total.

MAKING THE QUILT
Using a design wall, arrange the blocks alternating the plain blocks with the pieced ones. There are 9 blocks in each row and there are 10 rows. Move the blocks until the arrangement is harmonious. Sew the blocks into rows. Sew the rows together.

BLOCK ASSEMBLY DIAGRAM

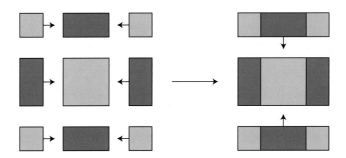

FINISHING THE QUILT

Press the quilt top. Seam the backing pieces using a ¼in (6mm) seam allowance to form a piece approx. 80in x 88in (203.2cm x 223.5cm).

Layer the quilt top, batting and backing and baste together (see page 164).

Quilt as preferred. The quilt shown was quilted in large-scale, random arabesques in an all-over pattern.

Trim the quilt edges and attach the binding (see page 165).

QUILT ASSEMBLY DIAGRAM

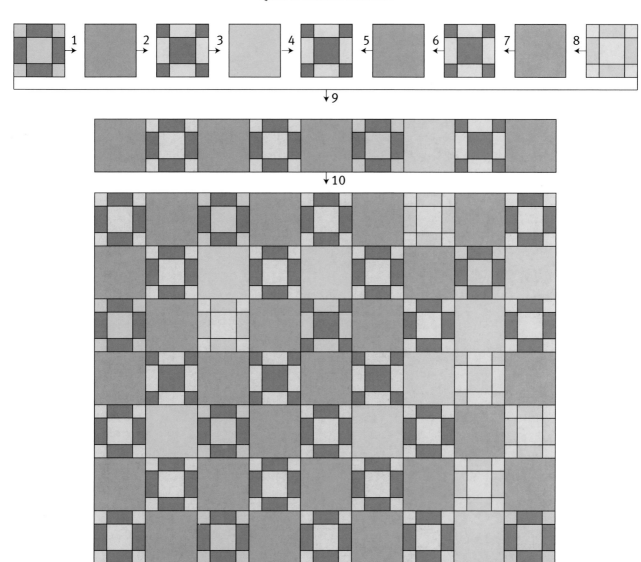

*Group 1 fabrics

PJ85PT
PJ86GY
PJ51PT
PJ84YE
PJ88PT
GP93PK

**Group 2 fabrics

GP71MT	GP70SK
GP01PT	GP70SF
GP59GY	BM60PK
GP59MV	BM37PT
GP70MT	BM43PK
GP70HY	BM53CD

***Group 3 fabrics

GP92PT
GP92PK
GP59TQ
BM60RD

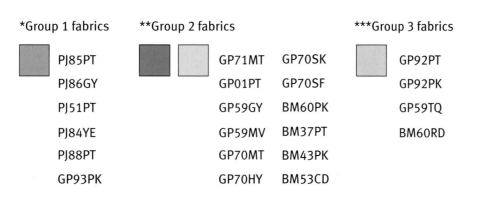

dark 9-patch *

Brandon Mably

This is Brandon's take on what is essentially a scrappy quilt. You don't need to place each fabric as in the original, and there is enough yardage to play with your colour choices a little.

SIZE OF FINISHED QUILT
72in x 80in (183cm x 203in)

MATERIALS
Fabrics calculated at minimum width of 40in (101.6cm) and are cut across the width, unless otherwise stated

Patchwork Fabrics
ROUND ROBIN
*Purple	BM63PU	½yd (45cm)
GLORY		
*Dark	PJ85DK	½yd (45cm)
LAKE BLOSSOM		
*Black	GP93BK	½yd (45cm)
JAPANESE CHRYSANTHEMUM		
*Antique	PJ41AN	¼yd (25cm)
*Red	PJ41RD	¼yd (25cm)
DREAM		
*Dark	GP148DK	¼yd (25cm)
VINE		
*Royal	GP151RY	¼yd (25cm)
HORSE CHESTNUT		
*Brown	PJ84BR	¼yd (25cm)
SOUND WAVES		
*Green	BM62GN	¼yd (25cm)
BRASSICA		
*Purple	PJ51PU	¼yd (25cm)

⅜yd (35cm) each of the following:
SPOT
**Royal	GP70RY
**Magenta	GP70MG
**Orange	GP70OR
**Cocoa	GP70CC
JUMBLE	
**Blue	BM53BL
**Ochre	BM53OC
GUINEA FLOWER	
**Brown	GP59BR
MILLEFIORE	
**Antique	GP92AN
PAPER FANS	
**Black	GP143BK
BAUBLES	
**Purple	BM61PU
**Black	BM61BK
SHARKS TEETH	
**Brown	BM60BR

CURLIQUE	
**Ochre	PJ87OC
ZIG ZAG	
**Black	BM43BK
MAD PLAID	
**Charcoal	BM37CC

Backing Fabric
BRASSICA
| Purple | PJ51PU | 5yd (4.6m) |

Binding
JUMBLE
| Blue | BM53BL | ¾yd (70cm) |

Batting
80in x 88in (203cm x 223.5cm)

Quilting Thread
Machine quilting thread

CUTTING OUT
Remove all selvedges before cutting out fabric.
There are three sizes of square and one size of rectangle in this quilt.
Cut each large square 8½in x 8½in (21.6cm x 21.6cm).
Cut each medium square 4½in x 4½in (11.4cm x 11.4cm).
Cut each small square 2½in x 2½in (6.4cm x 6.4cm).
Cut each rectangle 2½in x 4½in (6.4cm x 11.4cm).

Group 1 Fabrics (*)
These 10 fabrics are only used for the large squares: BM63PU, PJ85DK, GP93BK, PJ41AN, PJ41RD, GP148DK, GP151RY, PJ84BR, BM62GN and PJ51PU.

Group 2 Fabrics (**)
These 15 fabrics are used only for the medium and small squares, and for the rectangles: GP70RY, GP70MG, GP70OR, GP70CC, BM53BL, BM53OC, GP59BR, GP92AN, GP143BK, BM61PU, BM61BK, BM60BR, PJ87OC, BM43BK and BM37CC.

Large Squares
You need to cut out 45 large squares (plain blocks) in total. You can cut up to 8 squares from the Group 1 fabrics BM63PU, PJ85DK and GP93BK. You can cut up to 4 squares from each of the remaining Group 1 fabrics.

Medium and Small Squares and Rectangles
Cut the Group 2 ** fabrics to be sewn into pieced blocks. For each block, choose two fabrics. Cut one fabric into 1 medium square and 4 matching small squares. Cut the other fabric into 4 rectangles. Cut enough sets to make a total of 45 blocks.

Backing
From PJ41PU, cut 2 lengths approx. 88in (223.5cm) long. Remove the selvedges.

Binding
From BM53BL cut 9 strips 2½in (6.4cm) across the width of the fabric. Remove selvedges and sew together end to end.

MAKING THE BLOCKS
Use a ¼in (6mm) seam allowance throughout.
Follow the Block Assembly Diagram to sew the 9-patch blocks. Sew 45 blocks in total.

BLOCK ASSEMBLY DIAGRAM

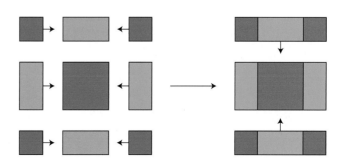

MAKING THE QUILT

Using a design wall, arrange the blocks so the plain blocks alternate with the pieced ones. There are 9 blocks in each row, and there are 10 rows. Move the blocks until the arrangement is harmonious. Sew the blocks into rows. Sew the rows together.

FINISHING THE QUILT

Press the quilt top. Seam the backing pieces using a ¼in (6mm) seam allowance to form a piece approx. 80in x 88in (203cm x 223.5cm). Layer the quilt top, batting and backing and baste together (see page 164). Quilt as preferred. The quilt shown was long-arm quilted with large-scale, random chevron patterns.

Trim the quilt edges and attach the binding (see page 165).

QUILT ASSEMBLY DIAGRAM

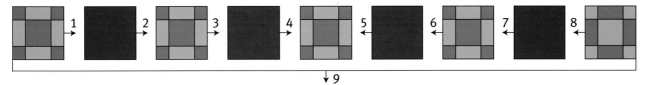

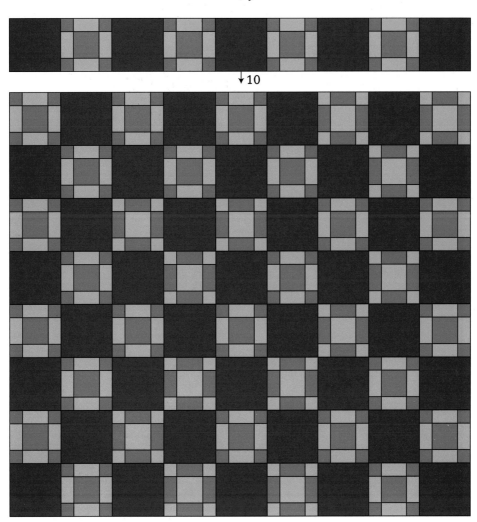

*Group 1 fabrics

BM63PU
PJ85DK
GP93BK
PJ41AN
PJ41RD
GP148DK
GP151RY
PJ84BR
BM62GN
PJ51PU

**Group 2 fabrics

GP70RY   BM61BK
GP70MG   BM60BR
GP70OR   PJ87OC
GP70CC   BM43BK
BM53BL   BM37CC
BM53OC
GP59BR
GP92AN
GP143BK
BM61PU

101

bold hexagons ✳✳✳

Kaffe Fassett and Liza Prior Lucy

At first glance this quilt appears to be simpler than it is. Hexagons are sewn into blocks made up of 6 hexagons with a 6-pointed star in the centre. Those blocks are sewn to each other using filler triangles in a way that makes the blocks swirl a bit clockwise. This glorious quilt is for expert machine sewers only. There are many Y-seams, and it requires very careful cutting and piecing. A simpler approach would be to use an English paper piecing technique and sew by hand, although this would be more time consuming. The design would be lovely scaled down.

SIZE OF FINISHED QUILT
98in x 112in (249cm x 284.5cm)

MATERIALS
Fabrics calculated at minimum width of 40in (101.6cm) and are cut across the width, unless otherwise stated

Patchwork Fabrics
SHOT COTTON
Coal   SC63   2¼yd (2m)
BIG STRIPE
Blue   BKKF05BL   2yd (1.85m)

1½yd (1.4m) each of the following:
ABORIGINAL DOT
Periwinkle   GP71PE
MILLEFIORE
Blue   GP92BL
SOUND WAVES
Green   BM62GN

1yd (90cm) each of the following:
BROAD STRIPE
Blue   WBSBL
SQUIGGLE
Green   PWKF05GR
RAKED
Cobalt   PWKF04CB

SPOT
Black   GP70BK   ¾yd (70cm)

½yd (45cm) each of the following:
ABORIGINAL DOT
Iris   GP71IR
SPOT
Sapphire   GP70SP
JUMBLE
Blue   BM53BL

¼yd (25cm) each of the following:
ABORIGINAL DOT
Charcoal   GP71CL
Plum   GP71PL
SPOT
Peacock   GP70PC

Backing Fabric
MILLEFIORE
Blue   GP92BL   9¼yd (8.5m)

Batting
106in x 120in (269cm x 305cm)

Binding
ABORIGINAL DOT
Periwinkle   GP71PE   1yd (1m)

Quilting Thread
Machine quilting thread

Template Plastic or Cardboard

TEMPLATES

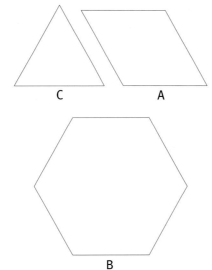

Three additional large templates D, E and F are needed for the outside edges of the quilt. Measurements are given overleaf to construct these or you can download the full-size templates at www.berrypublishing.co.uk. Include the grain-line arrows on your drawings. You will need sheets of A3 paper.

CUTTING OUT
Remove all selvedges before cutting out fabrics.
Make templates for the three shapes that make up the blocks (Templates A, B and C).
Download or draw the three shapes (Templates D, E and F) that make up the filler shapes of the quilt perimeter. The measurements given in the Perimeter Template Diagram overleaf include ¼in (6mm) seam allowance.

Cutting Diamonds
Use diamond Template A. Cut strips 3⅛in (8cm) x width of fabric. You will get 10 diamonds from each strip and will need 270 in total. Placing a flat side of the template along the top and bottom of the strip, cut the following:
GP71PE – 3 strips to cut 27 diamonds.
GP70BK – 8 strips to cut 72 diamonds.
GP71IR – 3 strips to cut 27 diamonds.
GP70SP – 5 strips to cut 45 diamonds.
BM53BL – 5 strips to cut 45 diamonds.
GP71CL – 2 strips to cut 18 diamonds.
GP71PL – 2 strips to cut 18 diamonds.
GP70PC – 2 strips to cut 18 diamonds.

Cutting Hexagons
Pay special attention to cutting the Big Stripe fabric so that the hexagons match with either a brown stripe or a blue at the top and bottom. Do not try to make matching hexagons from any of the other fabrics. You will get 5 matching hexagons from each strip. For all other hexagon fabrics, you will get 6 from a strip. Use hexagon Template B. Cut strips 5¾in (14.6cm) x width of fabric. You will get 6 hexagons from each strip and will need 270 in total. Placing a flat side of the template along the top and bottom edges of the strip, cut the following:
BKKF05BL – 11 strips to cut 54 *matching* hexagons.
WBSBL – 6 strips to cut 36 hexagons. Pay attention to stripe direction. The hexagons do not need to match but the stripe must run horizontally from straight edge to straight edge (not point to point).
PWKF04CB – 6 strips to cut 36 hexagons.
PWKF05GR – 6 strips to cut 36 hexagons.
BM62GN – 9 strips to cut 54 hexagons.
GP92BL – 9 strips to cut 54 hexagons.

PERIMETER SHAPE DIAGRAMS

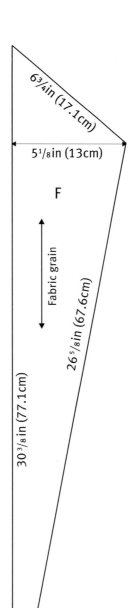

D
6⁷/₈in (17.5cm)
4³/₈in (11.1cm)
13¹/₂in (34.3cm)
18in (45.7cm)
Fabric grain

E
6⁵/₈in (17cm)
9³/₈in (23.8cm)
16in (40.6cm)
Fabric grain
5³/₄in (14.6cm)
6⁵/₈in (17cm)

F
6³/₄in (17.1cm)
5¹/₈in (13cm)
Fabric grain
26⁵/₈in (67.6cm)
30³/₈in (77.1cm)

Perimeter Template Measurements
Use the measurements in the diagrams to draw your own templates. Sizes given include ¼in (6mm) seam allowances.

Cutting Triangles
Use triangle Template C. From SC63 cut strips 3¹/₈in (8cm) x width of fabric. You will get 19 triangles from each strip. Placing the template on the strip, cut a triangle and then flip it back and forth to cut the triangles. From 20 strips cut a total of 362 triangles.

Cutting Perimeter Shapes
Three patch shapes in GP71PE are needed to fill the outer edges of the quilt. Pay attention to the grain lines shown on the diagrams and do *not* cut with fabric doubled. Note: you may prefer to wait until your quilt is assembled before cutting these fabric shapes. Some customizing and trimming may be needed.
From Template D cut 14. From Template E cut 8. From Template F cut 8.

Backing Fabric
Cut the yardage in thirds, approximately 3 yards to each length. Remove the selvedges.

Binding
From GP71PE cut 12 strips 2½in (6.4cm) x width of fabric.

MAKING THE BLOCKS
There are no simple ways of making this quilt top. The diagrams provided show how this one was made. Each block consists of 6 hexagons of a single fabric, 6 diamonds in two different fabrics and 6 triangles in shot cotton SC63.
Note: use Y-seams for the piecing, which means starting and stopping ¼in (6mm) from the beginning and end of each seam. Follow the Block Assembly Diagram and make 45 blocks in total.

BLOCK ASSEMBLY DIAGRAM

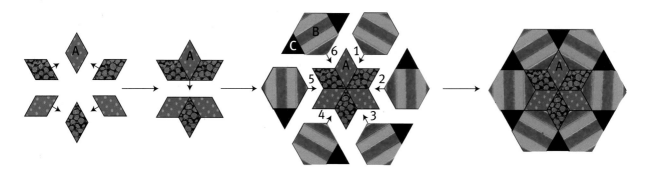

ASSEMBLING THE QUILT

Sew the blocks together in "rings." Each ring needs the addition of SC63 triangles (Template C) before proceeding to the next ring. The Ring Assembly Diagrams on page 106 give examples of how you could sew each ring – generally, work in a clockwise or anticlockwise direction.

Lastly, add the filler pieces around the edges of the quilt, as shown in the Final Quilt Assembly Diagram. Use Templates D, E and F to create straight sides to the quilt. On the sides of the quilt sew Template D fillers in position. On the top and bottom of the quilt sew the Template E fillers into place and then the Template F fillers. Some trimming of the shapes will be needed. Square up the quilt, making sure the corners are right angled.

FINISHING THE QUILT

Press the quilt top using spray starch. Sew the three lengths of backing fabric together side by side to make a piece approx. 108in x 120in (274cm x 305cm).

Layer the quilt top, batting and backing and baste together (see page 164). Quilt as preferred. The quilt shown was quilted in the ditch. The hexagons were quilted with free-form spirals, and the small diamonds quilted with a free-motion curving pattern. The shapes around the quilt edges have an all-over oval pattern. Trim the quilt edges and attach the binding (see page 165).

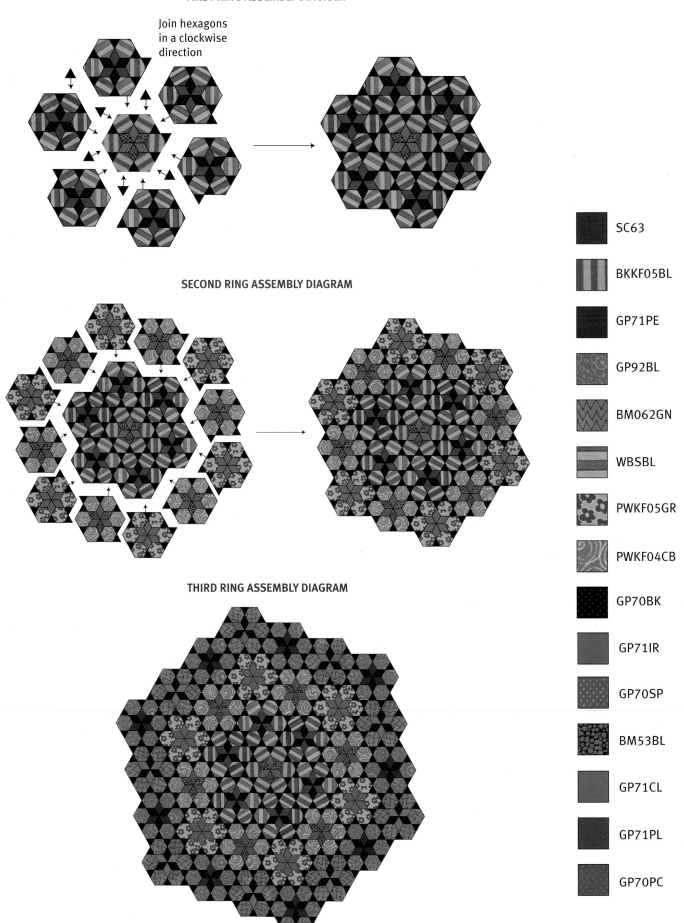

FIRST RING ASSEMBLY DIAGRAM

Join hexagons in a clockwise direction

SECOND RING ASSEMBLY DIAGRAM

THIRD RING ASSEMBLY DIAGRAM

SC63

BKKF05BL

GP71PE

GP92BL

BM062GN

WBSBL

PWKF05GR

PWKF04CB

GP70BK

GP71IR

GP70SP

BM53BL

GP71CL

GP71PL

GP70PC

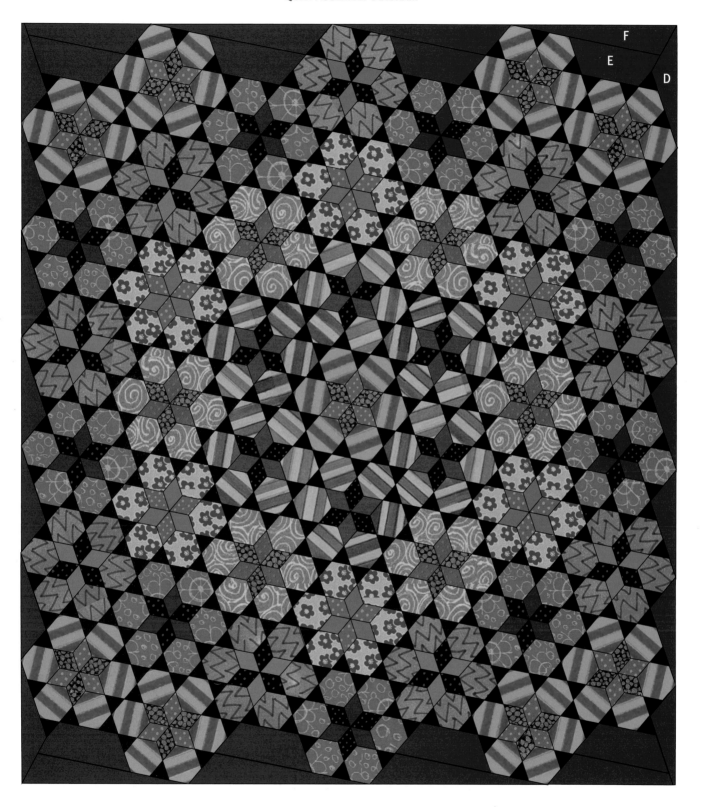

F
E
D

technicolour circles *

Kaffe Fassett

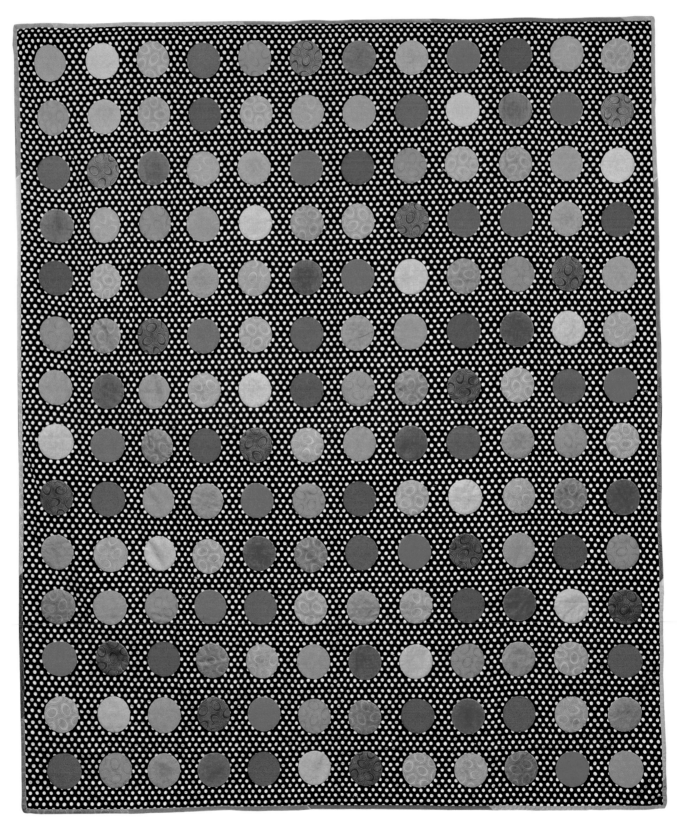

This quilt has been created as a relaxing hand-appliqué project, with multi-coloured Shot Cotton and Aboriginal Dot fabric circles appliquéd to a Spot Noir fabric background. If you prefer, it could be machine appliquéd, using the smaller template, and zig zag stitching the raw edges. A scrappy binding uses strips of the left-over coloured fabrics.

SIZE OF FINISHED QUILT
68in x 79in (172.7cm x 200.7cm)

MATERIALS
Fabrics calculated at minimum width of 40in (101.6cm) and are cut across the width, unless otherwise stated. The patchwork fabrics include sufficient for the scrappy binding.

Patchwork Fabrics
SPOT
Noir   GP70NR   4¾yd (4.4m)

⅜yd (35cm) each of the following:
ABORIGINAL DOT
Lime   GP71LM
Shocking   GP71SG
Gold   GP71GD
Orange   GP71OR
Wisteria   GP71WI
Canteloupe   GP71CA
Iris   GP71IR
SHOT COTTON
Pink   SC83
Cactus   SC92
Sprout   SC94
Sky   SC62
Jade   SC41

Backing Fabric
GLORY
Dark   PJ85DK   5yd (4.6m)

Batting
76in x 87in (193cm x 221cm)

Binding
For a scrappy binding, use leftover coloured fabrics, or ⅝yd (60cm) if using a single fabric

Fusible Interfacing (interlining)
White: medium to firm, non-woven, approx. 2yd (1.9m) of 36in (90cm) wide

Thread
Cotton sewing thread in colours to match appliqué fabrics
Machine quilting thread

Thick Card Stock
For circle appliqués

Spray starch
Hand sewing needle

TEMPLATES

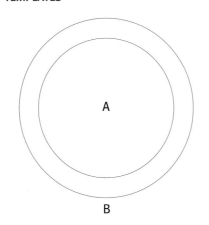

CUTTING OUT
Appliqué Shapes
The quilt is made up of 168 circular patch shapes (Template A) in mixed patchwork fabrics. They are bonded with smaller circles of fusible interfacing (Template B), as a lining and to give a firm edge when turning the hems on the circles.
Using Template A, from each of the 12 coloured patchwork fabrics, cut 14 circles 4½in (11.4cm) diameter for a total of 168. Reserve a 2½in (6.4cm) x width of fabric strip from each fabric for the binding.
Using Template B, cut 168 circles 3½in (9cm) from the fusible interfacing.

Background Fabric
Cut the length of GP70NR in half across the width to make 2 pieces approx.

84in (213.4cm) long. Do not remove selvedges.

Backing Fabric
Cut PJ85DK into 2 pieces about 87in x 40in (221cm x 101.6cm).

Binding
Using the remainder of the appliqué fabrics, cut a strip from each about 28in x 2½in (71cm x 6.4cm). Join the strips together to make a binding strip with a sewn length approx. 340in (863.6cm). If using a single-fabric binding, cut 8 strips 2½in (6.4cm) x width of fabric.

MAKING THE QUILT
Preparing Background Panels 1 and 2
The 2 background panels are appliquéd separately and sewn together later.
Note: The printed spots tend to run off-grain on this fabric, so trim the cut pieces at the top and bottom to ensure that the printed spots remain on the horizontal straight grain when the pieces are joined later. It is advisable to pattern match the panels by chalk marking. Do not trim or remove the selvedges at this point, as the extra fabric will help to pattern match the spots.

Making the Appliqué Circles
Follow the Circle Appliqué Diagram. Centre a fusible interfacing circle (Template B), onto the back of an appliqué fabric circle (Template A) and press to fuse. Snip regularly into the ½in (1.3cm) seam allowance, fold the seam allowance over and press (spray starch will give a crisp edge). Repeat to make 168 circles, placing each colour in a separate pile.
Note: If the background shows through the lighter fabric appliqués, cut and fuse an extra circle of fusible interfacing.

CIRCLE APPLIQUÉ DIAGRAM

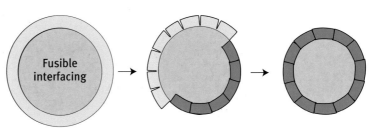

Fusible interfacing

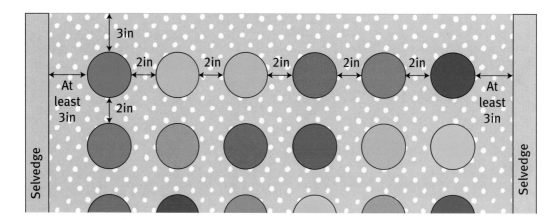

Sewing the Appliqué Circles

Refer to the Quilt Assembly Diagram for the colour placement of the appliqués. In the quilt shown, each horizontal row contains one each of the 12 coloured circles. Alternatively, decide on your own layout.

The circle positions run parallel with the background spots. Starting at the top-right corner of Panel 1, pin the first circle 3in (7.6cm) down from the top edge and at least 3in (7.6cm) in from the selvedge (see Circles Position Diagram). Pin the 5 other circles 2in (5cm) apart in a straight line across the width of the panel, following the line of the background spots. Pin the second row of circles 2in (5cm) down from the first row, and so on. It is helpful to work in batches of 3 to 4 rows at a time. Using matching thread, hand sew the circles into place with small slipstitches (see Tip).

Repeat with Panel 2, making sure the background spots and the appliqué circles are matched with Panel 1.

ASSEMBLING THE QUILT

Sew Panels 1 and 2 together along the marked seam line, with 2in (5cm) between the circles on the right side of Panel 1 and the left side of Panel 2. Make sure the appliqué circles are in line with one another. Trim all sides of the quilt evenly so it measures approx. 68½in x 79½in (174cm x 202cm).

FINISHING THE QUILT

Using a ¼in (6mm) seam, sew the 2 backing fabric pieces together and trim to a piece about 76in x 87in (193cm x 221cm).

Layer the quilt top, batting and backing together and baste (see page 164). Quilt as preferred.

The quilt shown was quilted in the ditch (or as close as possible to the appliqué) using thread colours to match the appliqués. If quilting on a domestic machine make sure that you baste it very well and closer than normal, about every 2in (5cm). Alternatively, the quilting can be done by hand.

Trim quilt edges and attach the binding (see page 165).

Tips

You could make the appliqué circles by gathering a 4½in (11.4cm) fabric circle over a 3½in (9cm) circle of card stock – see page 119 for method.

An embroidery hoop could be used to hand sew the circles in place. If you prefer machine work, you could attach them with a zig zag stitch around the edge.

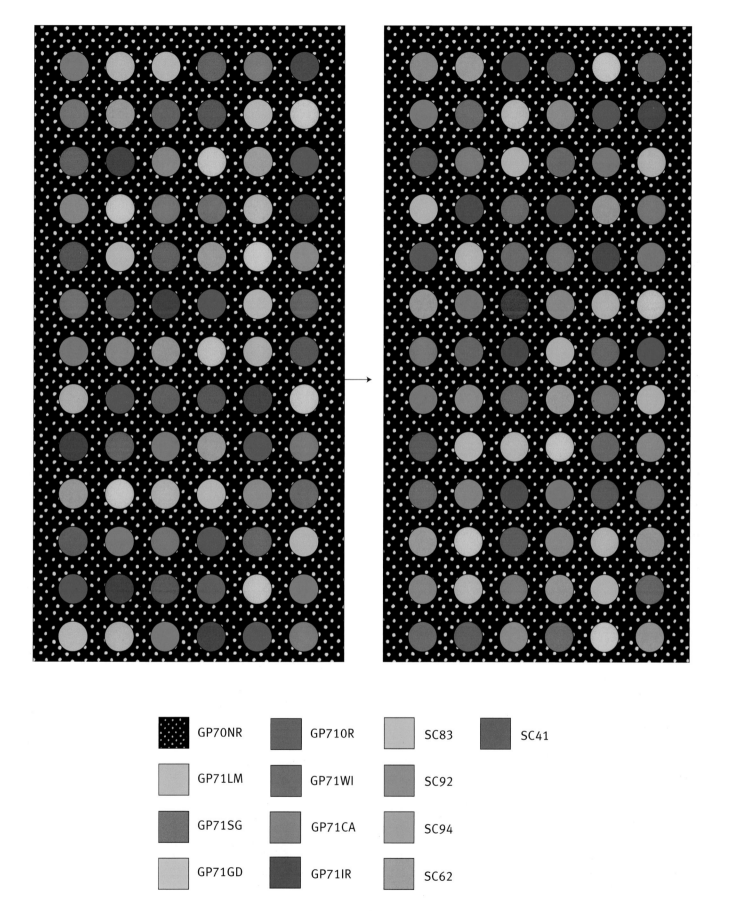

	GP70NR		GP710R		SC83		SC41
	GP71LM		GP71WI		SC92		
	GP71SG		GP71CA		SC94		
	GP71GD		GP71IR		SC62		

red ribbons ✱✱✱

Kaffe Fassett

We tried various methods to recreate the original quilt, and the one described here turned out to be the easiest. You could make this scrappy quilt in other ways, perhaps with string piecing on foundation paper. There is no right or wrong approach. Do what works best for you and enjoy the process in making this glorious, colour-saturated quilt.

SIZE OF FINISHED QUILT
68in x 68in (173 x 173cm)

MATERIALS
Fabrics calculated at minimum width of 40in (101.6cm) and are cut across the width, unless otherwise stated

Patchwork and Border Fabrics
1yd (90cm) each of the following:
ROMAN GLASS
Red   GP01RD
RAKED
Pumpkin   PWKF04PN
PAPERWEIGHT
Red   GP20RD

⅜yd (35cm) each of the following:
GUINEA FLOWER
Apricot   GP59AP
SPOT
Melon   GP70ME
Fuchsia   GP70FU
Shocking   GP70SG
Red   GP70RD
MILLEFIORE
Tomato   GP92TM
FERNS
Red   GP147RD
END PAPERS
Red   GP159RD
BAUBLES
Red   BM61RD
JUMBLE
Tangerine   BM53TN
Pink   BM53PK
ZIG ZAG
Warm   BM43WM
JAPANESE CHRYSANTHEMUM
Pink   PJ41PK
TULIP EXTRAVAGANZA
Pink   PJ89PK

Backing Fabric
SHAGGY
Red   PJ72RD   4½yd (4.2m)

Batting
76in x 76in (193cm x 193cm)

Binding
PAPERWEIGHT
Red   GP20RD   ⅝yd (60cm)

Quilting Thread
Machine quilting thread

Large Sheets of Sturdy Paper
To make paper patterns

MAKING PAPER PATTERNS
Cut the following pieces of paper to use as patterns – see Paper Patterns Diagram. For the triangles it is easiest to cut a square to the size given and then cut this in half once along the diagonal. The sizes given here include ¼in (6mm) seam allowances. Note that triangle B and triangle C are used in the quilt centre and also in the triangle border.
Centre square: 14⅝in x 14⅝in (37.1cm x 37.1cm).
Right-angled triangle A: short legs each 10⅞in (27.6cm).
Right-angled triangle B: short legs each 15in (38.1cm).
Right-angled triangle C: short legs each 20⅞in (53cm).

PAPER PATTERNS DIAGRAM

Cut sizes of paper patterns (seam allowances included)

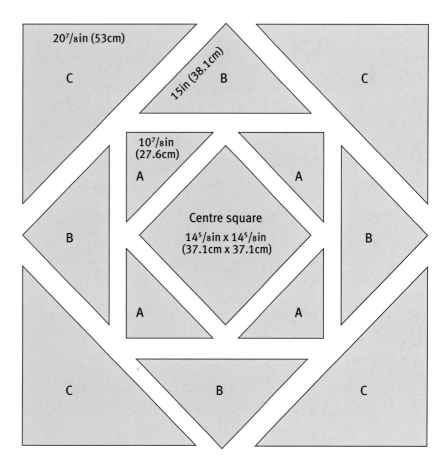

113

CUTTING OUT

Remove all selvedges before cutting out fabric.

Borders

The theoretical lengths of border strips needed are given *but we strongly advise* waiting until your quilt centre is complete before cutting the specific lengths, in case your quilt size is different from ours.
Inner border: From GP01RD, cut 7 strips each 1¾in (4.5cm) wide x width of fabric. Sew end to end. Cut 2 lengths each 60½in (154cm) and 2 lengths each 63½in (161.3cm).
Middle border: From PWKF04PN, cut 7 strips each 1½in (3.8cm) wide x width of fabric. Sew end to end. Cut 2 lengths each 63½in (161.3cm) and 2 lengths each 65½in (166.4cm).
Outer border: From GP20RD, cut 7 strips 2in (5cm) wide x width of fabric. Sew end to end. Cut 2 lengths 65½in (166.4cm) and 2 lengths 68½in (174cm).

Quilt Centre

This is a true scrappy quilt, so cut all the patchwork fabrics in random widths from 1¼in–2¼in (3.2cm–5.7cm) x width of fabric.

Backing

From PJ72RD cut 2 pieces approximately 76in (193cm) long.

Binding

From GP20RD) cut 8 strips 2½in (6.4cm) x width of fabric.

PIECING THE SHAPES DIAGRAMS

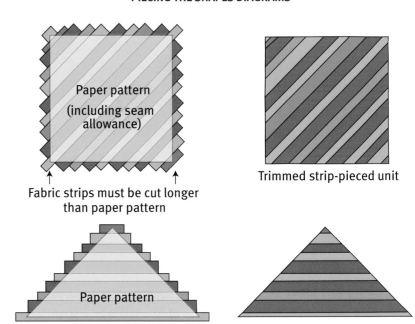

Paper pattern (including seam allowance)

Fabric strips must be cut longer than paper pattern

Trimmed strip-pieced unit

Paper pattern

QUILT CENTRE ASSEMBLY DIAGRAM

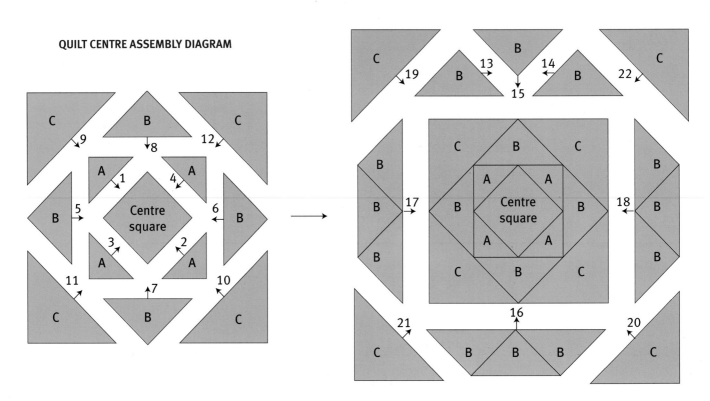

MAKING THE QUILT

Use a ¼in (6mm) seam allowance throughout. Refer to your paper patterns to cut the fabric strips, cutting them about 1in (2.5cm) longer than the pattern (see Piecing the Shapes Diagrams).
For the triangles, start at the base (the long side) of each triangle (so the fabric strips run parallel), sewing strips together randomly. Check to make sure the piece you are sewing is bigger than your paper pattern. It is best to use the wider strips as the first and last strips on a shape, as they will get trimmed down the most. When sewing strips together, alternate the direction you sew each seam, to help keep the patchwork un-bowed. Press strip-pieced units well.

Make 1 square bigger than the centre square paper pattern.
Make 4 triangles bigger than paper pattern A.
Make 16 triangles bigger than paper pattern B.
Make 8 triangles bigger than paper pattern C.
Cut out the shapes by placing the paper pattern on top of the patchwork shape, cutting with a quilting ruler and rotary cutter (seam allowances are included in the paper patterns). Stay stitch the two bias edges (short legs) on each triangle by sewing about ⅛in (3mm) from the edge. Do not tug the fabric as you feed it gently under the needle.

ASSEMBLING THE QUILT

Using the Quilt Centre Assembly Diagram as a guide, sew the 4 A triangles to the centre square. Add the 4 B and then the 4 C triangles.
For the outer B and C triangles, sew 3 B triangles together as shown in the diagram, and sew to the top of the quilt. Repeat this on the other three sides. Add the final 4 C triangles to each corner.
For the borders follow the Border Assembly Diagram. Sew the shorter GP01RD strips to the sides of the quilt, and the longer ones to the top and bottom. Repeat with the PWKF04PN border strips and then with the GP20RD border strips.

BORDER ASSEMBLY DIAGRAM

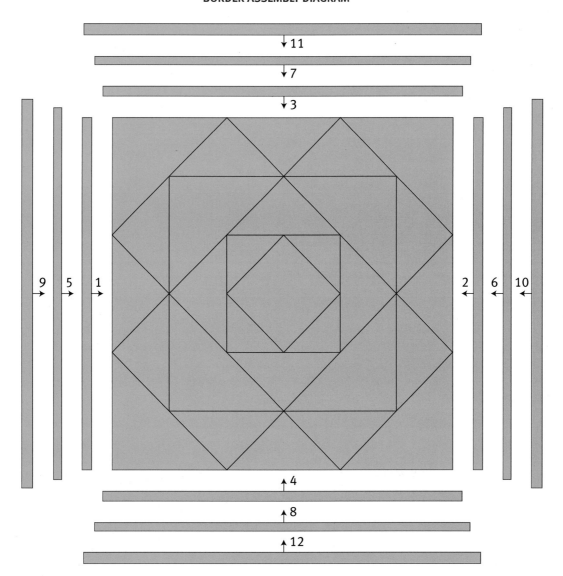

FINISHING THE QUILT

Press the quilt top. Seam the backing pieces together using a ¼in (6mm) seam allowance and trim to make a piece approx. 76in x 76in (193cm x 193cm). Layer the quilt top, batting and backing and baste together (see page 164). Quilt as preferred. The quilt shown was long-arm quilted in an all-over pattern of a loose arabesque design. Trim the quilt edges and attach the binding (see page 165).

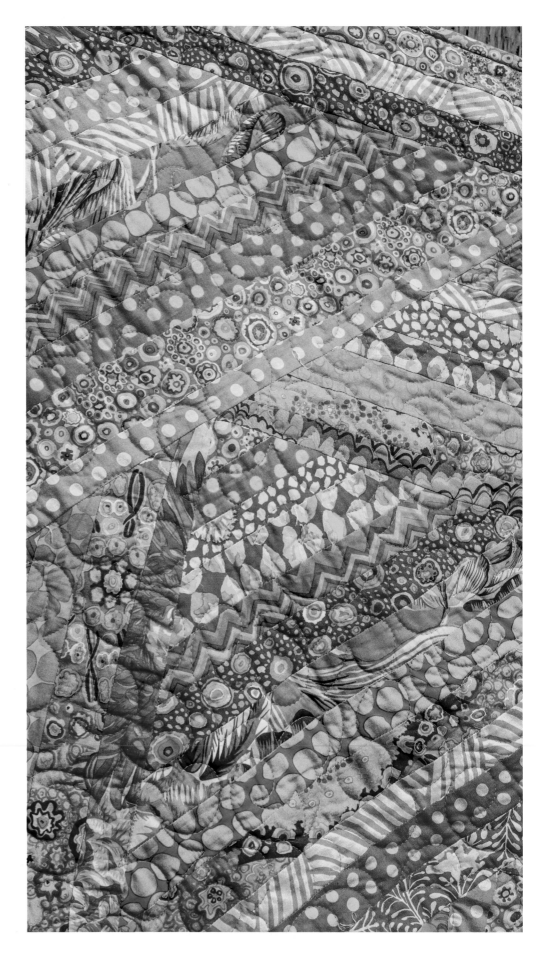

red stars ***

Kaffe Fassett

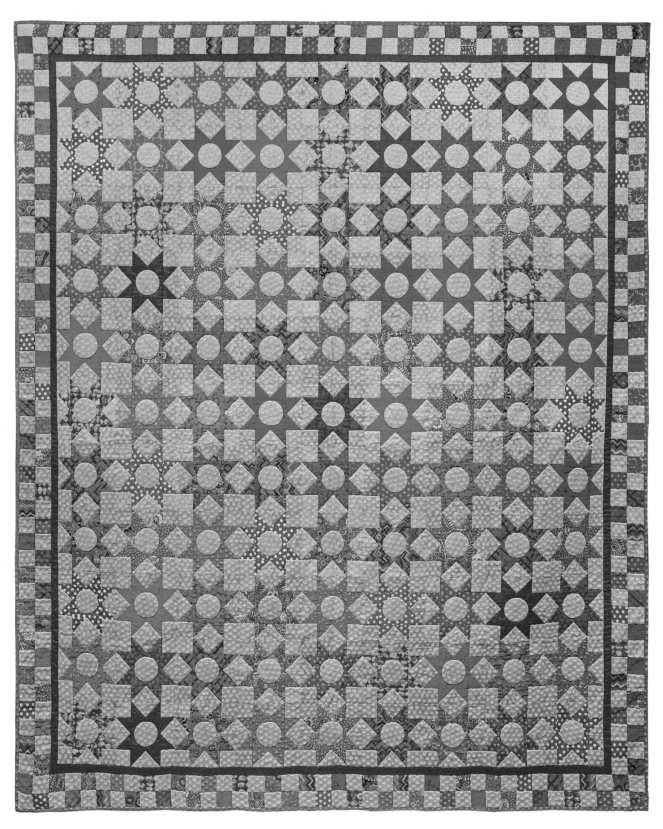

The Star Blocks in this quilt can be made as in the photo or with a scrappy layout, using all the red and pink fabrics in the Materials list below. The turquoise Spot fabric is used as a contrast for the circular centre of each Star Block and the background of the blocks. A mixture of red/pink fabrics and the Spot fabric make up the outer checkerboard border.

SIZE OF FINISHED QUILT
82in x 98in (208.5cm x 249cm)

MATERIALS
Fabrics calculated at minimum width of 40in (101.6cm) and are cut across the width, unless otherwise stated

Patchwork and Border Fabrics
SPOT
Turquoise   GP70TQ   7yd (6.4m)
Shocking   GP70SG   ½yd (45cm)
ABORIGINAL DOT
Red   GP71RD   ⅞yd (80cm),
includes ⅜yd (35cm) for narrow border

½yd (45cm) each of the following:
SPOT
Red   GP70RD
JUMBLE
Tangerine   BM53TN
ABORIGINAL DOTS
Shocking   GP71SG

⅜yd (35cm) each of the following:
BAUBLES
Red   BM61RD
MILLEFIORE
Tomato   GP92TM
GUINEA FLOWER
Apricot   GP59AP
ZIG ZAG
Warm   BM43WM
MAD PLAID
Red   BM37RD
SPOT
Fuchsia   GP70FU
Paprika   GP70PP
Tomato   GP70TM
JUMBLE
Pink   BM53PK
ABORIGINAL DOT
Orange   GP71OR
FERNS
Red   GP147RD
PAPERWEIGHT
Pink   GP20PK

Backing Fabric
CARPET
Red   GP001RD   2½yd (2.3m)
or 7yd (6.4m) of standard width

Binding
SPOT
Shocking   GP70SG   ¾yd (70cm)

Batting
90in x 106in (229cm x 269.5cm)

Quilting Thread
Machine quilting thread

Thick Card Stock
For circle appliqués

Spraystarch
Hand sewing needle

TEMPLATES

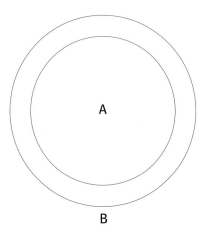

PATCHES

The quilt is composed of a central panel of 99 Star Blocks, a narrow border and a pieced checkerboard border. Each Star Block is made up of a 4½in x 4½in (11.4cm x 11.4cm) square of a red/pink, 4 squares 2½in x 2½in (6.4cm x 6.4cm) of turquoise GP70TQ and 8 half-square triangle (HST) units 2½in x 2½in (6.4cm x 6.4cm) using the same red/pink and turquoise GP70TQ. A 3in (7.6cm) diameter circle (finished) of turquoise GP70TQ is then appliquéd to the centre of each block.

The checkerboard border is made up of 2½in x 2½in (6.4cm x 6.4cm) squares, alternating turquoise GP70TQ and the various red/pinks.

CUTTING OUT

Remove all selvedges before cutting out fabric. All of the patches can be cut from strips cut across the width of the fabric. Cut strips as you go along. If you want a scrappier layout, you may want to use more of the red/pinks that you prefer and fewer of others.

Star Blocks

Centre squares: From each of the 17 red/pink fabrics cut 1 strip 4½in (11.4cm) across the width. A strip will give you up to 8 squares 4½in x 4½in (11.4cm x 11.4cm) . Cut 99 squares in total.
To make the quilt shown cut the following squares: 8 squares of GP70RD; 7 squares each of GP70SG, BM53TN, GP71SG; 6 squares each of BM61RD, GP92TM, GP59AP, BM43WM, BM37RD and 5 squares each of GP70FU, GP70PP, GP70TM, BM53PK, GP71OR, GP71RD, GP147RD, GP20PK.

Corner squares: From GP70TQ, cut 25 strips 2½in (6.4cm) across the width. Cut each strip into 2½in x 2½in (6.4cm x 6.4cm) squares (16 per strip). You need 396 squares in total.

Half-square triangle (HST) units: Each Star Block has 8 HST units 2½in x 2½in (6.4cm x 6.4cm) (unfinished), which need to use the same red/pink fabric as the centre square. The units can be made using a two-at-once method, with 1 square 2⅞in x 2⅞in (7.3cm x 7.3cm) of GP70TQ and 1 square 2⅞in x 2⅞in

(7.3cm x 7.3cm) of red/pink. Each Star Block will need 4 squares of GP70TQ and 4 squares of a red/pink.
Cut each 2⅞in (7.3cm) strip cut across the width to give up to 13 squares 2⅞in x 2⅞in (7.3cm x 7.3cm). Cut the following number of strips and squares: 31 strips to give 396 squares in GP70TQ.
3 strips each to give 28 squares each of GP70SG, BM53TN, GP71SG.
2 strips each to give 24 squares each of BM61RD, GP92TM, GP59AP, BM43WM, BM37RD.
2 strips each to give 20 squares each of GP70FU, GP70PP, GP70TM, BM53PK, GP71OR, GP71RD, GP147RD, GP20PK.

Circle Appliqués

Use Template A to mark and cut out 3in (7.6cm) diameter circles from thick card stock. Cut out several of each. Use Template B to mark and cut 99 fabric circles 4in (10.2cm) in diameter in GP70TQ (this allows for a ½in (1.3cm) seam allowance).

Narrow Border

From GP71RD cut 9 strips 1½in (3.8cm) across the width. Sew the strips together end to end and then cut 2 strips 88½in (224.8cm) long and 2 strips 74½in (189.2cm) long.

Checkerboard Border

From GP70TQ, cut 11 strips 2½in (6.4cm) across the width. When cross-cut, each strip will give you 16 squares 2½in x 2½in (6.4cm x 6.4cm). You need 172 squares in total.
From each red/pink fabric cut 1 strip 2½in (6.4cm) across the width. Cut a total of 172 squares 2½in x 2½in (6.4cm x 6.4cm). You can cut roughly equal numbers from each fabric, or cut more squares from some and fewer from others.

Backing

Remove the selvedges.
If using extra-wide backing, from GP001RD cut a piece 90in x 106in (229cm x 269.5cm).
If using standard-width backing, from GP001RD cut 2 lengths approx. 106in (269.5cm) long. From the remaining fabric, cut 3 strips 11in (28cm) across the width.

Binding

From GP70SG, cut 10 strips 2½in (6.4cm) across the width. Remove the selvedges and sew together end to end.

MAKING THE QUILT

Use ¼in (6mm) seam allowances throughout.

Star Blocks

For each Star Block, from the same red/pink fabric take 1 square 4½in x 4½in (11.4cm x 11.4cm) and 4 squares 2⅞in x 2⅞in (7.3cm x 7.3cm). From GP70TQ, take 4 squares 2½in x 2½in (6.4cm x 6.4cm) and 4 squares 2⅞in x 2⅞in (7.3cm x 7.3cm).
Make 8 HST units using the 2⅞in x 2⅞in (7.3cm x 7.3cm) squares and using the two-at-once method shown in the Half-Square Triangle Unit Diagram. HST units need to be 2½in x 2½in (6.4cm x 6.4cm) square (unfinished).
Assemble each block as shown in the Star Block Assembly Diagram (also see Tip). Make 99 blocks in total.

Once the Star Blocks are made, appliqué a GP70TQ circle to the centre of each block as follows (see Circle Appliqué Diagram). Use the Template A card circle to mark a circle in the centre of a GP70TQ circle. Remove the card and work a circle of running stitches a fraction outside the marked circle. Replace the card circle (Template A) and pull up the running stitches to gather the fabric circle around the card. Spray starch, press and then remove the card.
Using tiny slipstitches and matching thread, sew the appliqué circle to the centre of the Star Block. Repeat for all Star Blocks.

Tip

To avoid possible problems with the fit of the outer checkerboard border later, check your Star Blocks are 8½in x 8½in (21.6cm x 21.6cm) square (unfinished). If not, adjust your seam allowance accordingly.

Checkerboard Border

Sew the GP70TQ and red/pink 2½in x 2½in (6.4cm x 6.4cm) squares into 2-patch units (see Border Assembly Diagram). Make 172 2-patch units in total.

Make 2 strips of 45 units for each side of the quilt. Make 2 strips of 41 units for the top and bottom of the quilt.

MAKING THE QUILT

Lay out the quilt centre with the Star Blocks in 11 rows of 9 blocks each, as shown in the Quilt Assembly Diagram. (Or choose your own arrangement, using a design wall to help with placing.) Sew the blocks into rows and then sew the rows together.

Add the narrow border strips, sewing the longer strips to the sides of the quilt and then the shorter strips to the top and bottom.

Add the checkerboard border, sewing the longer strips to the sides of the quilt and then the shorter strips to the top and bottom. To retain the checkerboard effect around the quilt corners, orientate the strips as shown in the Quilt Assembly Diagram.

FINISHING THE QUILT

Press the quilt top. If using extra-wide backing, use the 90in x 106in (229cm x 269.5cm) piece.

If using standard-width backing, using a ¼in (6mm) seam allowance, sew the 3 narrow strips together end to end and then trim to 11in x 106in (28cm x 269.5cm). Sew this narrow panel between the 2 wider pieces to form a backing approx. 90in x 106in (229cm x 269.5cm).

Layer the quilt top, batting and backing and baste together (see page 164).

Quilt as preferred. The quilt shown was quilted in the ditch around all Star Blocks, along the sashing horizontal and vertical seams and between the chequerboard units. It was echo quilted around the appliqué circles.

Trim the quilt edges and attach the binding (see page 165).

HALF-SQUARE TRIANGLE UNIT DIAGRAM

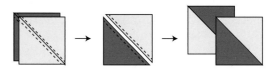

STAR BLOCK ASSEMBLY DIAGRAM

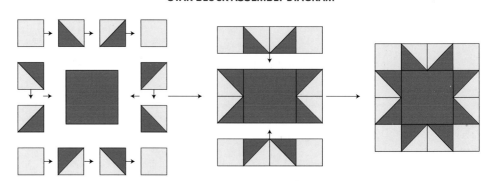

CIRCLE APPLIQUÉ DIAGRAM

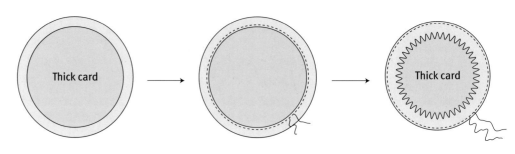

Thick card — Thick card

BORDER ASSEMBLY DIAGRAM

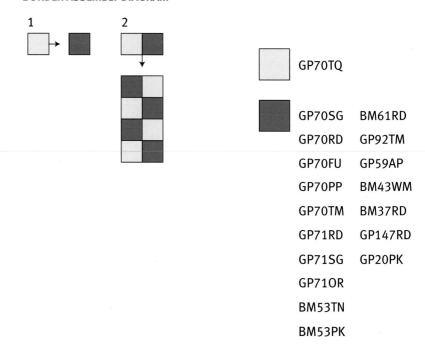

GP70TQ	
GP70SG	BM61RD
GP70RD	GP92TM
GP70FU	GP59AP
GP70PP	BM43WM
GP70TM	BM37RD
GP71RD	GP147RD
GP71SG	GP20PK
GP71OR	
BM53TN	
BM53PK	

QUILT ASSEMBLY DIAGRAM

tippecanoe and tyler too ***

Liza Prior Lucy

There are only three fabrics in this quilt! Kaffe's Regimental Stripes fabric has various patterns of stripes across the width. The clever fussy cutting of the fabric to create a variety of spinning stars makes the quilt look even more complex than it is.

SIZE OF FINISHED QUILT
80in x 80in (203.2cm x 203.2cm)

MATERIALS
Fabrics calculated at minimum width of 40in (101.6cm) and are cut across the width, unless otherwise stated

Patchwork Fabrics

LILAC		
Dark	PJ68DK	3¾yd (3.4m)
REGIMENTAL STRIPES		
Blue	GP163BL	2⅛yd (2m)
SPOT		
Black	GP70BK	2¼yd (2.3m)

Backing Fabric

CURLIQUE		
Blue	PJ87BL	6¼yd (5.7m)

Binding

SPOT		
Black	GP70BK	⅝yd (60cm)

Batting
88in x 88in (223.5cm x 223.5cm)

Quilting Thread
Machine quilting thread

TEMPLATE

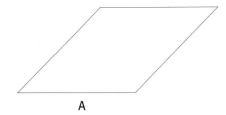

A

CUTTING OUT

From PJ68DK cut all of the pieces lengthwise (parallel to the selvedge).

Border

Cut a top and a bottom border strip each 6½in x 80½in (16.5cm x 204.5cm). Cut two side border strips each 6½in x 68½in (16.5cm x 174cm).

Sashing

From the remaining PJ68DK, cut 64 rectangles each 3½in x 9½in (9cm x 24cm). Cut 24 corner posts each 3½in x 3½in (9cm x 9cm).

Sashing Setting Triangles

From the remaining PJ68DK cut 4 squares each 5½in x 5½in (14cm x 14cm). On each square, cut across both diagonals to make 4 triangles (for a total of 16).

Block Triangles

From GP70BK, remove selvedges and cut 10 strips 2¾in (7cm) across the fabric width. Cut each of these strips into 14 squares each 2¾in x 2¾in (7cm x 7cm). Cut each square diagonally once to make 2 triangles from each square. You will need a total of 256 of these small triangles.

From GP70BK, cut 12 strips 3½in (9cm) across the fabric width. Cut each of these strips into 11 squares each 3½in x 3½in (9cm x 9cm). Cut each square diagonally once to make 2 triangles from each square. You will need a total of 256 of these large triangles.

Block Diamonds

The diamonds are cut from the Regimental Stripes (GP163BL) fabric. The stripes are hand-painted and imperfect so it would be hard to make all 8 star points in a block identical. Even so, the stars will swirl imperfectly, but nicely. In GP163BL, fold the fabric in half, wrong sides together, selvedge to selvedge (see Fabric Preparation Diagram). Cut off the selvedges and line up the stripes so those facing you and those underneath match as closely as possible. Cut into 3 units (Unit 1, Unit 2 and Unit 3), each 21in (53.4cm) deep plus one unit (Unit 4) 10in (25.5cm) deep. Press the units well. Cut Unit 1, 2 and 3 into strips from folded edge to raw edge, each 2⅜in (6cm)

wide. Each 21in (53.4cm) unit will yield 8 matching strips (Units 1, 2 and 3) – see Diamond Cutting Diagram. (Unit 4 will be used for the extra diamonds needed for the partial blocks.)

Starting with Unit 1, place Template A on the first strip and cut out. Place the template on the next strip, starting in the same spot as the first strip, and cut out. Continue in this way to cut 8 matching diamonds. Separate the 8 diamonds on the top layer from the 8 diamonds on the bottom layer and set aside. You now have enough to make 2 star blocks. Repeat this process until you have 10 matching sets from Unit 1.

Repeat this process with Unit 2 and Unit 3. Start in a slightly different spot on these units to make these stars a bit different from the Unit 1 stars. Continue in this way until you have 25 matching sets to make 25 whole blocks. Keep the spare diamonds in their matching sets as these are needed for the half blocks and quarter blocks.

The shorter Unit 4 is cut using the same process (see Diamond Cutting Diagram – Unit 4). These diamonds are used for the half blocks and quarter blocks around the edges of the quilt. The 12 half blocks each need 4 matching diamonds. The 4 corner blocks each need 2 matching diamonds.

Backing

From PJ87BL cut 2 pieces 90in (229cm) long. Cut the remaining piece lengthwise into three 11in (28cm) strips. Remove selvedges. Sew the 3 narrow strips end to end and trim to 90in (229cm).

Binding

From GP70BK cut 9 strips each 2½in (6.4cm) x width of fabric.

MAKING THE BLOCKS

Use a ¼in (6mm) seam allowance throughout.

For each whole block choose a matched set of 8 GP163BL diamonds, 8 large GP70BK triangles and 8 small GP70BK triangles. Follow the Block Assembly Diagram to piece together.

For each half-block choose 4 matching diamonds, 4 large triangles and 4 small triangles (see Partial Blocks Assembly Diagram).

For each corner block choose 2 matching diamonds, 2 large triangles and 2 small triangles (see Partial Blocks Assembly Diagram).

Follow the diagrams to make 25 whole blocks, 12 half blocks and 4 corner blocks.

MAKING THE QUILT

Arrange the blocks randomly and follow the Quilt Assembly Diagram on page 00, sewing the blocks together "on point" in diagonal rows, alternating with sashing strips. Sew the diagonal rows between the blocks with sashing strips, corner posts and sashing triangles. Sew the diagonal rows together and then add the partial blocks in each corner of the quilt. Once the centre is complete, add the side border strips and then the top and bottom border strips.

FINISHING THE QUILT

Press the quilt top. Seam the backing pieces, using a ¼in (6mm) seam allowance. Sew the narrow, pieced strip between the two wider pieces to form a piece approx. 90in x 90in (229cm x 229cm).

Layer the quilt top, batting and backing and baste together (see page 164). Quilt as preferred. The quilt shown was quilted "in the ditch" outlining all stars and sashing. The interior diamonds of the stars have curvilinear patterns quilted within, while the border flowers are randomly outline quilted.

Trim the quilt edges and attach the binding (see page 165).

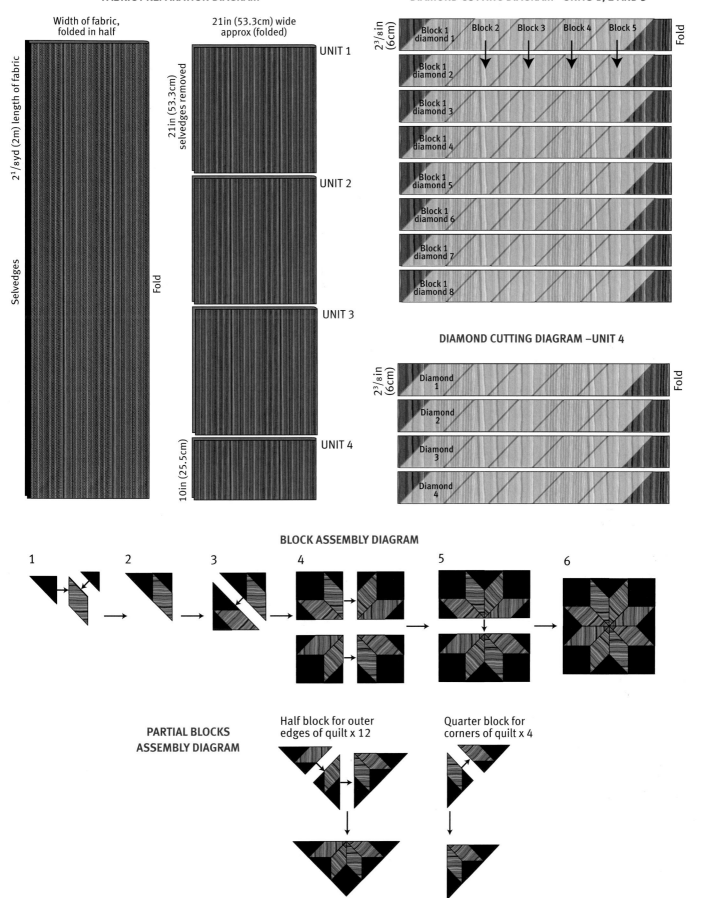

FABRIC PREPARATION DIAGRAM

Width of fabric, folded in half

21in (53.3cm) wide approx (folded)

$2^{1}/_{8}$yd (2m) length of fabric

21in (53.3cm) selvedges removed

10in (25.5cm)

Selvedges

Fold

UNIT 1

UNIT 2

UNIT 3

UNIT 4

DIAMOND CUTTING DIAGRAM –UNITS 1, 2 AND 3

$2^{3}/_{8}$in (6cm)

Block 1 diamond 1

Block 2   Block 3   Block 4   Block 5

Fold

Block 1 diamond 2

Block 1 diamond 3

Block 1 diamond 4

Block 1 diamond 5

Block 1 diamond 6

Block 1 diamond 7

Block 1 diamond 8

DIAMOND CUTTING DIAGRAM –UNIT 4

$2^{3}/_{8}$in (6cm)

Diamond 1

Diamond 2

Diamond 3

Diamond 4

Fold

BLOCK ASSEMBLY DIAGRAM

1   2   3   4   5   6

PARTIAL BLOCKS ASSEMBLY DIAGRAM

Half block for outer edges of quilt x 12

Quarter block for corners of quilt x 4

125

QUILT ASSEMBLY DIAGRAM

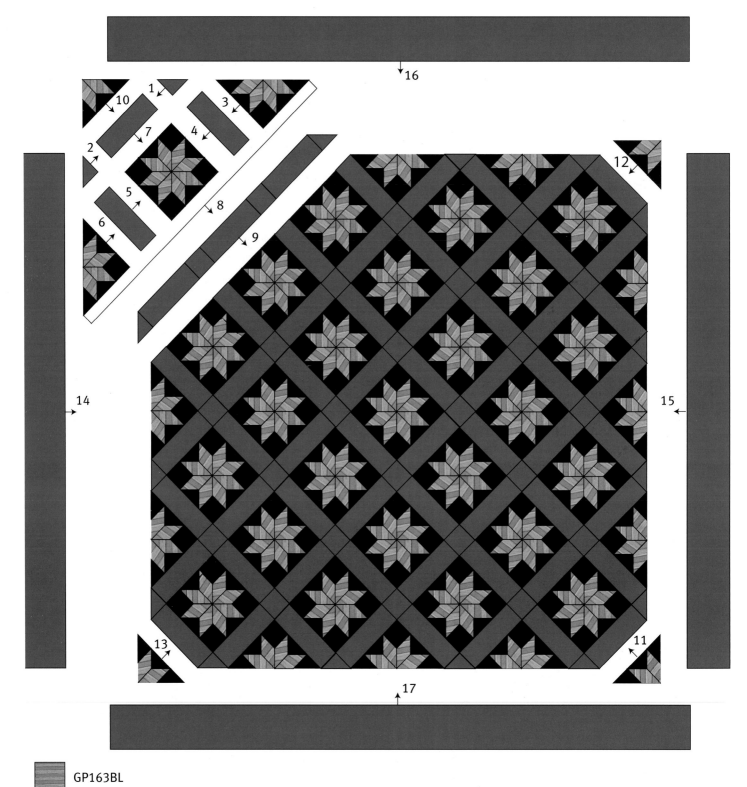

GP163BL

PJ68DK

GP70BK

dotty fans ***

Kaffe Fassett

This elegant design has fan blocks on point, floating on a Spot Soft background. The blocks are made using foundation paper piecing for the fan. Curved piecing is needed for the inner and outer curved sections. This is a scrappy quilt, and it isn't necessary to place each fabric as in the original to achieve the same effect. Arrange the blocks so that the colours are well spread and visually pleasing and there is an even distribution of red and pink fabrics.

SIZE OF FINISHED QUILT
68¾in x 78½in (174.5cm x 199.5cm)

MATERIALS
Fabrics calculated at minimum width of 40in (101.6cm) and are cut across the width, unless otherwise stated

Patchwork Fabrics
SPOT
Soft	GP70SF	5¼yd (4.8m)
Duck Egg	GP70DE	1m (90cm)
White	GP70WH	⅜yd (35cm)
Gold	GP70GD	⅜yd (35cm)
Noir	GP70NR	¼yd (25cm)
Ochre	GP70OC	⅜yd (35cm)
Lavender	GP70LV	¼yd (25cm)
Sky	GP70SK	⅜yd (35cm)
Tomato	GP70TM	⅜yd (35cm)
Teal	GP70TE	⅜yd (35cm)
China	GP70CI	⅜yd (35cm)
Melon	GP70ME	⅜yd (35cm)
Turquoise	GP70TQ	⅜yd (35cm)

JUMBLE
Fuchsia	BM53FU	⅜yd (35cm)
Pink	BM53PK	¼yd (25cm)
Turquoise	BM53TQ	⅝yd (55cm)
Tangerine	BM53TN	⅜yd (35cm)
White	BM53WH	¼yd (25cm)
Green	BM53GN	¼yd (25cm)
Candy	BM53CD	¾yd (70cm)
Orange	BM53OR	¼yd (25cm)

GUINEA FLOWER
White	GP59WH	⅜yd (35cm)
Yellow	GP59YE	¼yd (25cm)
Mauve	GP59MV	¼yd (25cm)
Grey	GP59GY	⅜yd (35cm)
Pink	GP59PK	½yd (45cm)
Turquoise	GP59TQ	⅜yd (35cm)

Backing
PAPER FANS
Contrast	GP143CO	5¼yd (4.8m)

Binding
JUMBLE
White	BM53WH	¾yd (70cm)

Batting
78in x 88in (198cm x 223.5cm)

Quilting Thread
Machine quilting thread

Thin paper or foundation paper piecing paper

TEMPLATES

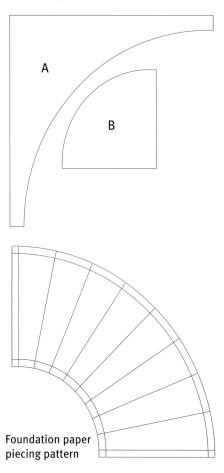

Foundation paper piecing pattern

PATCH SHAPES
The quilt centre is made up of 98 fan blocks. Each block consists of one fan unit (made with foundation paper piecing), one Template A patch (outer curve) and one Template B (inner curve) – see Block Layout Diagram. The "blades" of the fan are alternating light and dark fabrics. Side setting triangles and corner triangles are used to complete the outer edges of the quilt.

BLOCK LAYOUT DIAGRAM

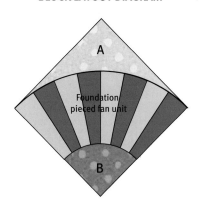

CUTTING OUT
Remove all selvedges before cutting out fabric.
Fan unit: Make 98 copies of the foundation pattern (to avoid distortion, make all copies directly from the book – not copies from copies). Note that the pattern on page 154 has already been reversed, ready for use.

Each fan unit has 8 blades – 4 dark and 4 light. Cut the patches for blades larger than needed in order to cover the strips on the foundation pattern with at least ¼in (6mm) extra all round. A cut size of 2½in x 5in (6.4cm x 12.7cm) for each blade patch is sufficient. Cut strips 2½in (6.4cm) x width of fabric and then sub-cut to length as needed.

All fan units are made the same way but there are 16 different colour combinations – see list below for the numbers of units to make, fabric combinations and numbers of blades to cut (refer to the quilt photo on page 127 for placement).

Cut out as follows:
8 units of GP70GD and GP59GY – 32 blades of each;
6 units of GP70NR and GP59MV – 24 blades of each ;
7 units of GP59PK and GP70SK – 28 blades of each;
7 units of GP59TQ and GP70WH – 28 blades of each;
8 units of BM53FU and GP59WH – 32 blades of each;
5 units of GP59YE and GP70CI – 20 blades of each;
2 units of BM53CD and GP70CI – 8 blades of each;

8 units of GP70TM and BM53CD –
32 blades of each;
4 units of GP59PK and BM53GN –
16 blades of each;
6 units of BM53OR and GP70LV –
24 blades of each;
5 units of BM53PK and GP70TE –
20 blades of each;
8 units of BM53TN and GP70TQ –
32 blades of each;
7 units of BM53TQ and BM53CD –
28 blades of each;
8 units using BM53TQ and GP70OC –
32 blades of each;
6 units of GP70ME and BM53WH –
24 blades of each;
3 units of GP70TE and GP70ME –
12 blades of each.

Template A: From GP70SF and using
Template A cut 98 patches.
Template B: From GP70DE and using
Template B cut 98 patches.
Setting triangles: From GP70SF cut
7 squares 11⅛in (28.3cm). Cut each
square in half along both diagonals to
make four triangles. You need a total of
26 setting triangles.
Corner triangles: From GP70SF cut 2
squares 5⅞in (15cm). Cut each square
in half once along the diagonal to make a
total of four corner triangles.

Backing Fabric
Cut GP143CO into 2 pieces each 40in x
90in (101.6cm x 229cm).

Binding
From BM53WH cut 9 strips 2½in (6.4cm)
across the width of the fabric.

MAKING THE BLOCKS
Use a ¼in (6mm) seam allowance
throughout.

Foundation Piecing a Fan Unit
See Basic Techniques on page 000 for
advice. Take a foundation paper pattern
and flip it over to the blank side – see
Foundation Piecing Diagram stages 1 to
4. Follow the numbered piecing order
shown on the pattern. Select the 8 blade
patches needed for a single unit. Take the
first blade patch and place it right side
up over the patch marked 1, making sure
it extends past the seam line on all sides
by at least ¼in (6mm). Take the second

FOUNDATION PIECING DIAGRAMS

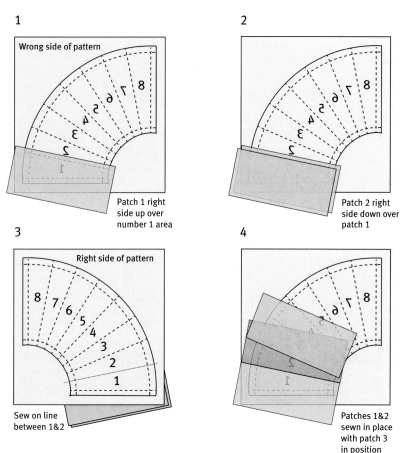

1 Wrong side of pattern — Patch 1 right side up over number 1 area

2 — Patch 2 right side down over patch 1

3 Right side of pattern — Sew on line between 1&2

4 — Patches 1&2 sewn in place with patch 3 in position

BLOCK ASSEMBLY DIAGRAM

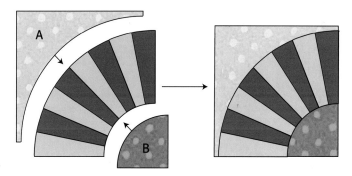

blade patch, place it right side down on
blade 1 and pin in place. Carefully flip
the paper pattern over so the print side
is uppermost and sew along the line
between piece 1 and piece 2.
Flip the pattern back to the non-printed
side. Fold the paper pattern out of the
way, trim the seam allowance to ¼in
(6mm) and press piece 2 into place.
Repeat this process to add the rest of the
pieces, alternating the fabrics.
Trim the fan unit to the outer line on the

pattern and remove the paper pattern.
Make all 98 fan units using the same
method.

Assembling a Block
Sew the Template A and Template B
patches to a pieced fan unit using curved
piecing and a *scant* ¼in (6mm) seam
allowance (see Block Assembly Diagram).
Snip into the curved seams at intervals
and then press the block. Repeat to
complete all 98 blocks.

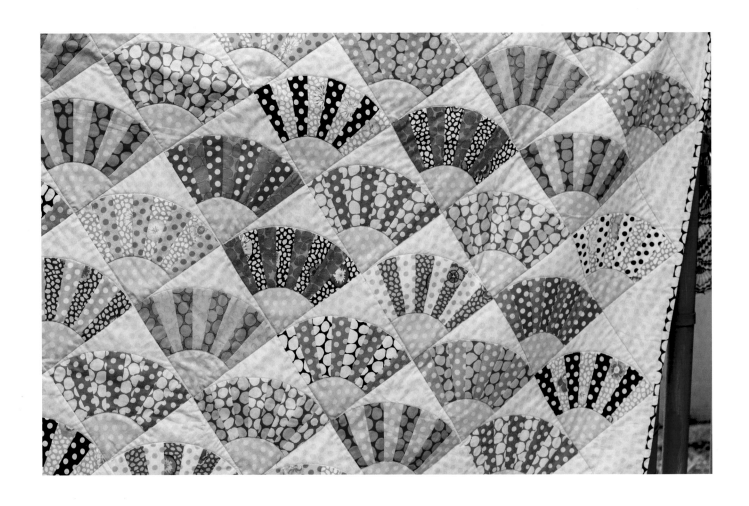

MAKING THE QUILT

Lay out the blocks following the Quilt Assembly Diagram, with the fan blocks arranged in 14 diagonal rows in an on-point layout. Alternatively, arrange the blocks in your own order – a design wall will help with placement.

Sew the blocks together in diagonal rows, adding setting triangles to the end of each row. Sew the rows together and then sew the corner triangles in place to complete the quilt.

FINISHING THE QUILT

Press the quilt top. Sew the backing pieces together to make a piece approx. 78in x 90in (198cm x 229cm).
Layer the quilt top, batting and backing and baste together (see page 164).
Quilt as preferred. The quilt shown was quilted in the ditch around all of the blocks and filler triangles. Echo quilting was worked just beyond the upper and lower curved edges of the fans.
Trim quilt edges and attach the binding (see page 165).

BACKGROUND FABRICS	LIGHT FABRICS	DARK FABRICS
GP70SF	G70WH	GP70GD
GP70DE	GP70OC	GP70NR
	GP70LV	*GP70TM
	GP70SK	GP70TE
	*GP70CI	BM53FU
	*GP70ME	BM53TQ
	GP70TQ	BM53TN
	BM53PK	BM53OR
	BM53WH	GP59YE
	BM53GN	GP59PK
	BM53CD	GP59TQ
	GP59WH	
	GP59MV	
	GP59GY	

* fabrics used as both light and dark

130

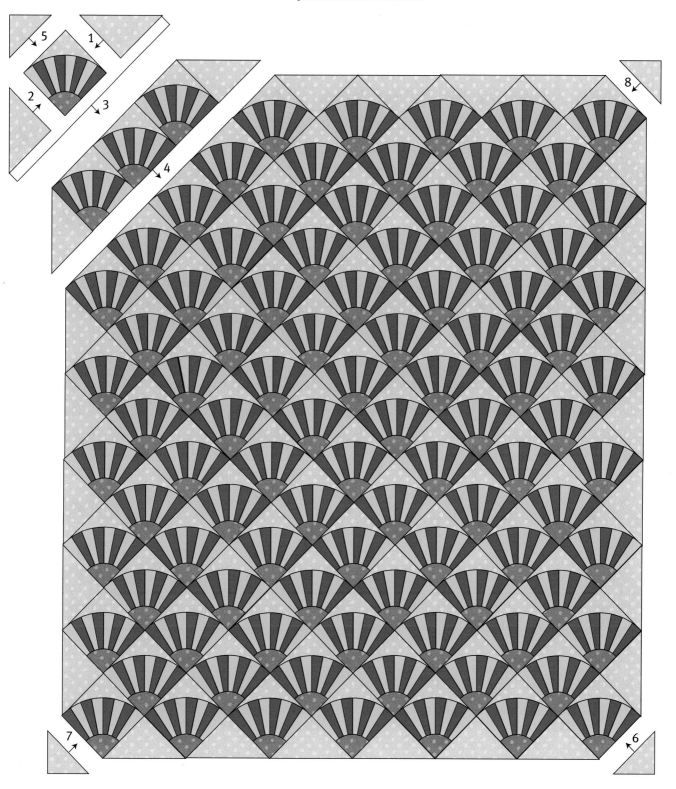

badge of honour ***

Kaffe Fassett

This exquisite quilt, made in the traditional light and shade log cabin pattern, showcases red, white and blue fabrics. The use of the dark Aboriginal Dot Orchid fabric highlights the formation of the cross pattern. Assorted medium and light fabrics have been used for the pale half of each unit. The narrow strips are created using a foundation paper piecing method, and the instructions assume experience with this technique. Fabric quantities are generous to allow sufficient for foundation piecing.

SIZE OF FINISHED QUILT
63in x 63in (160cm x 160cm)

MATERIALS
Fabrics calculated at minimum width of 40in (101.6cm) and are cut across the width, unless otherwise stated

Patchwork Fabrics
Dark Fabric
ABORIGINAL DOT

Orchid	GP71OD	6¼yd (5.75yd)

Medium Fabrics
ABORIGINAL DOT

Chocolate	GP71CL	¾yd (70cm)
Charcoal	GP71CC	1yd (90cm)
Iris	GP71IR	1yd (90cm)
SPOT		
Sapphire	GP70SP	¾yd (70cm)
Tobacco	GP70TO	⅝yd (60cm)
ROMAN GLASS		
Red	GP01RD	¾yd (70cm)
FERNS		
Red	GP147RD	⅜yd (35cm)
GUINEA FLOWER		
Blue	GP59BL	½yd (45cm)

Light Fabrics
ABORIGINAL DOT

Mint	GP71MT	1yd (90cm)
Cream	GP71CR	1yd (90cm)
Taupe	GP71TA	¾yd (70cm)
SPOT		
Duck Egg	GP70DE	⅝yd (60cm)
Peach	GP70PH	⅜yd (35cm)
PAPERWEIGHT		
Sludge	GP20SL	1yd (90cm)

Backing Fabric

Whirligig	GP166BK	4⅛yd (3.8m)

Batting
71in x 71in (180cm x 180cm)

Binding
ABORIGINAL DOT
Orchid   GP71OD   ⅝yd (60cm)

Quilting Thread
Machine quilting thread

Thin paper or foundation paper piecing paper
196 copies

TEMPLATE

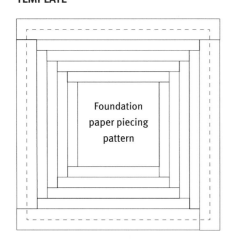

Foundation paper piecing pattern

PATCHES

There are 49 blocks in the quilt, in 12 different colourways. Each block is made up of 4 foundation-pieced log cabin units. The dark diagonal half of the unit is created with GP71OD, while the paler diagonal half is made up of medium and light fabrics (see Unit Layout Diagram). Note that strips 1 and 2 use the same fabric, 5 and 6 use the same fabric and so on. The narrow strips or "logs" are added clockwise around the centre square.

CUTTING OUT

Remove all selvedges before cutting out fabric.

Make 196 copies of the foundation pattern (to avoid distortion, make all copies directly from the book – not copies from copies). Note that the pattern on page 161 has already been reversed, ready for use.

Cut the patches larger than needed in order to cover the areas on the foundation pattern with at least ¼in (6mm) extra all around. Cut sizes are given in the table below (⅜in larger all round than the finished size). Cut strips for the "logs" from the width of the fabric, and sub-cut to length as needed.

Patch	Cut size for foundation piecing
Centre	2¾in (7cm) square
Strip 1	1in x 2¾in (2.5cm x 7cm)
Strip 2	1in x 3in (2.5cm x 7.6cm)
Strip 3	1in x 3in (2.5cm x 7.6cm)
Strip 4	1in x 3¼in (2.5cm x 8.3cm)
Strip 5	1in x 3¼in (2.5cm x 8.3cm)
Strip 6	1in x 3½in (2.5cm x 9cm)
Strip 7	1in x 3½in (2.5cm x 9cm)
Strip 8	1in x 3¾in (2.5cm x 9.5cm)
Strip 9	1in x 3¾in (2.5cm x 9.5cm)
Strip 10	1in x 4in (2.5cm x 10.2cm)
Strip 11	1in x 4in (2.5cm x 10.2cm)
Strip 12	1in x 4¼in (2.5cm x 10.8cm)
Strip 13	1in x 4¼in (2.5cm x 10.8cm)
Strip 14	1in x 4½in (2.5cm x 11.4cm)
Strip 15	1in x 4½in (2.5cm x 11.4cm)
Strip 16	1in x 4¾in (2.5cm x 12cm)
Strip 17	1in x 4¾in (2.5cm x 12cm)
Strip 18	1in x 5¼in (2.5cm x 13.3cm)
Strip 19	1in x 5¼in (2.5cm x 13.3cm)
Strip 20	1in x 5¾in (2.5cm x 14.6cm)

Unit centres: From assorted medium fabrics, cut 2¾in (7cm) strips across the width of the fabric and sub-cut into 2¾in (7cm) squares. You will need 196 in total. Cut the following numbers:
4 GP70SP; 80 GP71IR; 32 GP71CC; 16 GP01RD; 8 GP71CL; 24 GP147RD; 32 GP70TO.

Dark strips: From GP71OD cut the dark strips 3, 4, 7, 8, 11, 12, 15, 16, 19 and 20, cutting the strips 1in (2.5cm) x the length given in the table above.

Light strips: The paler half of the units generally follow an alternating light/medium pattern of strips. From assorted medium and light fabrics cut patches for the light logs 1, 2, 5, 6, 9, 10, 13, 14, 17 and 18, cutting the strips 1in (2.5cm) deep x the length given in the table above. See the Unit Colourways Diagram on page 136 for the fabrics used.

Backing
From GP166BK cut 2 pieces 72in (183cm).

Binding
From GP71OD cut 7 strips 2½in (6.4cm) across the width of the fabric.

UNIT LAYOUT DIAGRAM

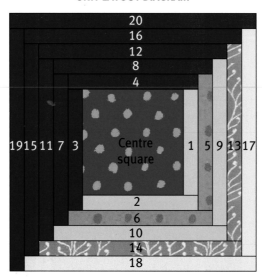

134

FOUNDATION PIECING DIAGRAM

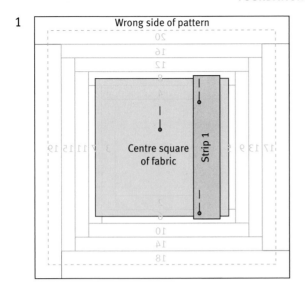

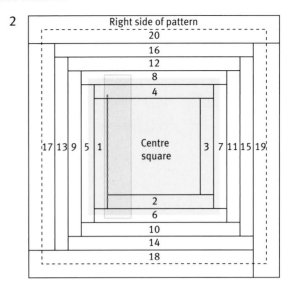

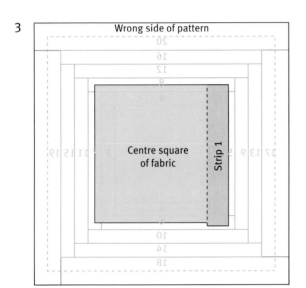

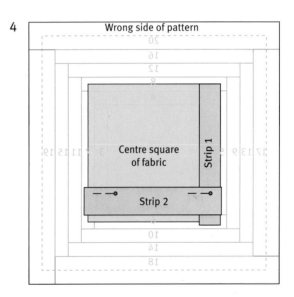

MAKING THE LOG CABIN UNITS

Each block is made up of 4 log cabin units, each made with foundation piecing.

Take a foundation pattern and flip it over to the blank side. Pin a centre square of fabric right side up over the marked centre square, making sure it extends past the seam line on all sides by at least ¼in (6mm). Take a Strip 1 of light fabric and pin it right side down on the centre square, making sure it extends past the seam line on all sides by at least ¼in

(6mm) (see Foundation Piecing Diagram 1). Carefully flip the paper pattern over so the print side is uppermost and sew along the line between the centre square and Strip 1 (diagram 2). Flip the pattern back to the non-printed side. Fold the paper pattern out of the way, trim the seam allowance to ¼in (6mm) and press the strip into place (diagram 3). Repeat this process to add Strip 2 (this will be the same fabric as strip 1).

Continue in this way to add all of the strips, following the number order and

changing fabrics as needed. Trim seam allowances as you go. Once all strips have been added, trim the fabric unit to the outer solid line on the pattern – it should be 5in (12.7cm) square at this stage, and includes a seam allowance. Leave the paper pattern in place for the moment.

Make another 3 log cabin units using the same fabrics. You can remove the papers after the 4 units for a block have been made, or leave them in place until the block is sewn together.

UNIT COLOURWAYS DIAGRAM

Unit Block 1 (1 block)

Unit Block 2 (8 blocks)
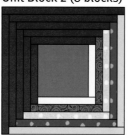

Unit Block 3 (4 blocks)

Unit Block 4 (4 blocks)
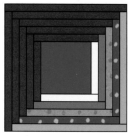

Unit Block 5 (2 blocks)
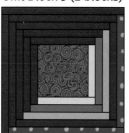

Unit Block 6 (2 blocks)
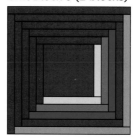

Unit Block 7 (4 blocks)
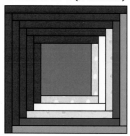

Unit Block 8 (8 blocks)
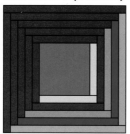

Unit Block 9 (4 blocks)

Unit Block 10 (8 blocks)
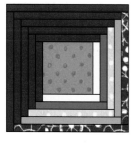

Unit Block 11 (2 blocks)
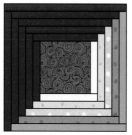

Unit Block 12 (2 blocks)

Use foundation piecing to make all of the blocks. Follow the Unit Colourway Diagrams for the 12 different blocks, making the following number of blocks:
1 of block 1 (centre block of quilt);
8 of block 2; 4 of block 3; 4 of block 4;
2 of block 5; 2 of block 6; 4 of block 7;
8 of block 8; 4 of block 9; 8 of block 10:
2 of block 11; 2 of block 12.

ASSEMBLING A BLOCK
Take 4 matching log cabin units and arrange them so a cross shape is formed by the light fabrics. Sew the units in pairs and press. Now sew the pairs together and press (see Block Assembly Diagram). Repeat to make 49 blocks in total.

ASSEMBLING THE QUILT
Lay out the blocks in 7 rows of 7 blocks each, as shown in the Quilt Assembly Diagram. There is a regular pattern to the block order and the numbers on the blocks of the Assembly Diagram refer to the numbered blocks (left). Sew the blocks into rows and then sew the rows together.

FINISHING THE QUILT
Press the quilt top. Sew the backing pieces together to make a piece approx. 72in x 72in (183cm x 183cm).
Layer the quilt top, batting and backing and baste together (see page 164).
Quilt as preferred. The quilt shown was quilted in the ditch of all large blocks and centre squares.
Trim the quilt edges and attach the binding (see page 165).

BLOCK ASSEMBLY DIAGRAM

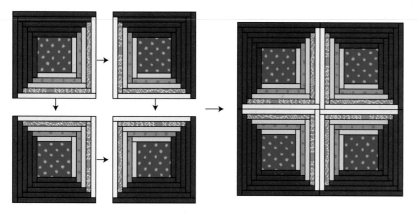

136

QUILT ASSEMBLY DIAGRAM

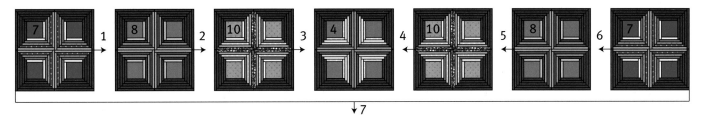

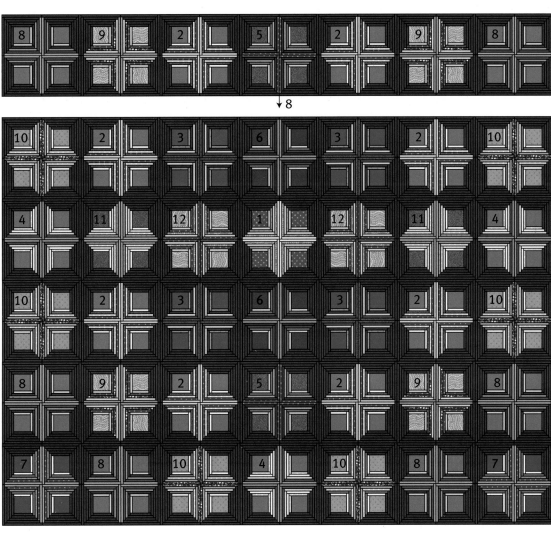

DARK FABRIC

GP71OD

MEDIUM FABRICS

GP71CL

GP70TO

GP71CC

GP01RD

GP71IR

GP147RD

GP70SP

GP59BL

LIGHT FABRICS

GP71MT

GP70PH

GP71CR

GP20SL

GP71TA

GP70DE

green boxes ***

Kaffe Fassett

If you're up for a challenge then this eye-catching quilt is for you. The Courtyard Steps-style blocks are made with templates to create a diamond shape, each framed with Spot Pond (GP70PO). These diamonds are joined together with Y-seams into larger hexagon blocks. Filler triangles are used to create straight edges on the quilt.

SIZE OF FINISHED QUILT
60in x 56in (152.5cm x 142cm)

MATERIALS
Fabrics calculated at minimum width of 40in (101.6cm) and are cut across the width, unless otherwise stated

Patchwork Fabrics
ABORIGINAL DOT
Lilac	GP71LI	⅞yd (80cm)

GUINEA FLOWER
Pink	GP59PK	¼yd (25cm)

FERNS
Green	GP147GN	¼yd (25cm)
Turquoise	GP147TQ	⅜yd (35cm)

ROMAN GLASS
Emerald	GP01EM	¼yd (25cm)

JUPITER
Malachite	GP131MA	¼yd (25cm)

SHARKS TEETH
Green	BM60GN	¼yd (25cm)

PAPERWEIGHT
Algae	GP20AL	¼yd (25cm)

JUMBLE
Turquoise	BM53TQ	¼yd (25cm)
Green	BM53GN	¼yd (25cm)

SPOT
Pond	GP70PO	1¾yd (1.6m)
Lichen	GP70LN	¼yd (25cm)
Peach	GP70PH	¼yd (25cm)
Turquoise	GP70TQ	¼yd (25cm)
Shocking	GP70SG	¼yd (25cm)
Duck Egg	GP70DE	¼yd (25cm)
Teal	GP70TE	¼yd (25cm)
Lavender	GP70LV	⅜yd (35cm)

Backing Fabric
TREFOIL
Multi	GP167MU	3¾yd (3.5m)

Batting
68in x 64in (173cm x 162.5cm)

Binding
JUMBLE
Green	BM53GN	⅝yd (60cm)

Quilting Thread
Machine quilting thread

TEMPLATES

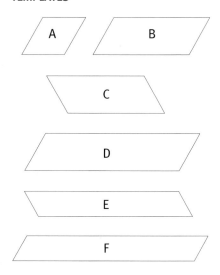

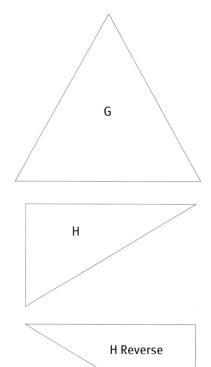

PATCH SHAPES
This quilt is made up of pieced diamonds, joined together in trios to form hexagon blocks. Setting triangles fill in at the sides of the quilt. The pieced diamonds are made from 6 templates, A, B, C, D, E and F – see Block Layout Diagram.

CUTTING OUT
Remove all selvedges before cutting out fabric. Make templates for the six shapes that make up a diamond block (Templates A, B, C, D, E and F). When using the templates to cut the fabric patches take care to place them correctly on the fabrics, so the arrow follows the fabric grain. You may wish to cut each block as you go.

Block Patches
Template A (centre patch only): Cut 1½in (3.8cm) strips across the width of the fabric. Using Template A cut the following numbers of patches (for block centres). You need a total of 73.
3 GP59PK; 6 GP147GN; 11 GP147TQ; 9 GP01EM; 8 GP131MA; 3 BM60GN; 7 GP20AL; 4 BM53TQ; 5 BM53GN; 6 GP70LN; 1 GP70PH; 1 GP70TQ; 2 GP70DE; 4 GP70TE and 3 GP70LV.

BLOCK LAYOUT DIAGRAM

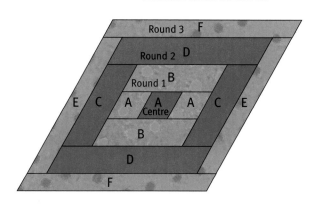

Template A (round 1): Cut 1½in (3.8cm) strips across the width of the fabric. Using Template A cut the following numbers of patches. You need a total of 146.
28 GP71LI; 12 GP59PK; 2 GP147TQ; 10 BM60GN; 6 BM53TQ; 2 BM53GN; 6 GP70LN; 14 GP70PH; 8 GP70TQ; 20 GP70SG; 6 GP70DE; 6 GP70TE and 26 GP70LV.

Template B: Cut 1½in (3.8cm) strips across the width of the fabric. Using Template B (round 1) cut the following numbers of patches (same as Template A round 1). You need a total of 146.
28 GP71LI; 12 GP59PK; 2 GP147TQ; 10 BM60GN; 6 BM53TQ; 2 BM53GN; 6 GP70LN; 14 GP70PH; 8 GP70TQ; 20 GP70SG; 6 GP70DE; 6 GP70TE and 26 GP70LV.

Template C: Cut 1½in (3.8cm) strips across the width of the fabric. Using Template C (round 2) cut the following numbers of patches. You need a total of 146.
6 GP59PK; 12 GP147GN; 22 GP147TQ; 18 GP01EM; 16 GP131MA; 6 BM60GN; 14 GP20AL; 8 BM53TQ; 10 BM53GN; 12 GP70LN; 2 GP70PH; 2 GP70TQ; 4 GP70DE; 8 GP70TE and 6 GP70LV.

Template D: Cut 1½in (3.8cm) strips across the width of the fabric. Using Template D (round 2) cut the following numbers of patches (same as Template C). You need a total of 146.
6 GP59PK; 12 GP147GN; 22 GP147TQ; 18 GP01EM; 16 GP131MA; 6 BM60GN; 14 GP20AL; 8 BM53TQ; 10 BM53GN; 12 GP70LN; 2 GP70PH; 2 GP70TQ; 4 GP70DE; 8 GP70TE and 6 GP70LV.

Template E: Cut 1in (2.5cm) strips across the width of the fabric. Using Template E (round 3) cut 146 from GP70PO.

Template F: Cut 1in (2.5cm) strips across the width of the fabric. Using Template F (round 3) cut 146 from GP70PO.

Quilt Edge Patches
Template G: Cut a 6¾in (17.1cm) strip across the width of the fabric. Using Template G cut 4 patches from GP71LI. Rotate the template 180 degrees alternately for economical cutting.

Template H: Cut a 4⅛in (10.5cm) strip across the width of the fabric. Using Template H cut 10 patches from GP71LI. Rotate the template 180 degrees alternately for economical cutting (see Template H Cutting Diagram).

Template H Reverse: Cut a 4⅛in (10.5cm) strip across the width of the fabric. Using Template H Reverse cut 10 patches from GP71LI.

Backing Fabric
Cut GP167MU into two halves 40in x 64in (101.6cm x 162.5cm). Trim one piece to 29in (73.7cm) wide.

Binding
From BM53GN cut 7 strips 2½in (6.4cm) across the width of the fabric.

TEMPLATE H CUTTING DIAGRAM

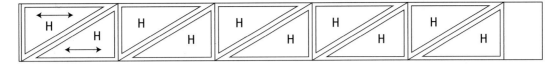

MAKING THE BLOCKS

Use a ¼in (6mm) seam allowance throughout. Assemble a block as shown in the Block Assembly Diagram, adding shapes to the sides of the unit and then the top and bottom, and continuing in 3 rounds. Refer to the Quilt Assembly Diagram for fabric placement to make a total of 73 pieced diamonds.

Using Y-seams (that is, starting and stopping stitching ¼in (6mm) from the beginning and end of each seam), join 3 diamonds to form a hexagon block (see Hexagon Assembly Diagram). Repeat to make 23 hexagons in total. The remaining 4 diamonds will be used to fill in the quilt sides

MAKING THE QUILT

Lay out the hexagon blocks in rows as in the Quilt Assembly Diagram. Place the four pieced diamonds on each end of row 2 and row 4. Using Y-seams, sew triangles H and H reverse to the hexagons at the top and bottom of the quilt. Now sew the hexagons together and then sew the rows together.

Add triangles G to the sides of the quilt.

FINISHING THE QUILT

Press the quilt top. Sew the backing pieces together using a ¼in (6mm) seam allowance to form a piece approx. 68in x 64in (173cm x 162.5cm). Press the seam open. Layer the quilt top, batting and backing and baste together (see page 164).

Quilt as preferred. The quilt shown was quilted in the ditch around each element of diamond blocks and also in the ditch of the outer shapes.

Trim the quilt edges and attach the binding (see page 165).

BLOCK ASSEMBLY DIAGRAMS

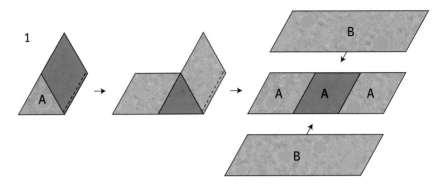

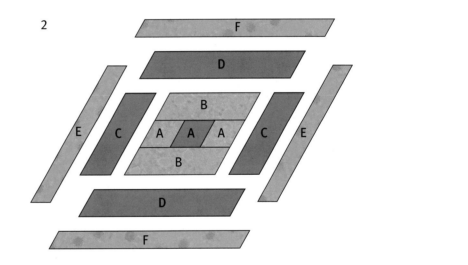

HEXAGON ASSEMBLY DIAGRAM

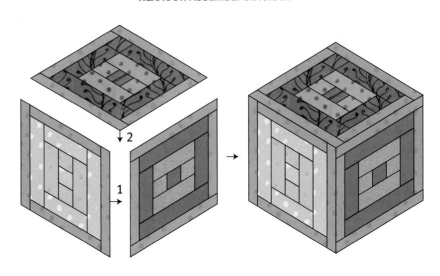

141

QUILT ASSEMBLY DIAGRAM

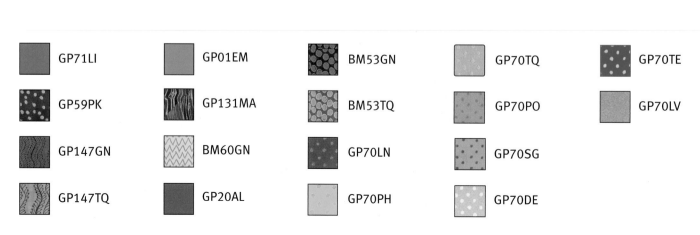

	GP71LI		GP01EM		BM53GN		GP70TQ		GP70TE
	GP59PK		GP131MA		BM53TQ		GP70PO		GP70LV
	GP147GN		BM60GN		GP70LN		GP70SG		
	GP147TQ		GP20AL		GP70PH		GP70DE		

giant blocks **

Kaffe Fassett

This eye-catching quilt is a great example of the Tumbling Blocks pattern.

SIZE OF FINISHED QUILT
70in x 86in (178cm x 218.5cm)

MATERIALS
Fabrics calculated at minimum width of 40in (101.6cm) and are cut across the width, unless otherwise stated

Patchwork Fabrics
DarkFabrics
ABORIGINAL DOT

Orchid	GP71OD	¾yd (70cm)

MILLEFIORE

Dark	GP92DK	1yd (90cm)

FERNS

Black	GP147BK	½yd (45cm)

SPOT

Black	GP70BK	½yd (45cm)

Medium Fabrics
ABORIGINAL DOT

Charcoal	GP71CC	⅜yd (40cm)

MILLEFIORE

Antique	GP92AN	¾yd (70cm)

JUMBLE

Ochre	BM53OC	½yd (45cm)

FERNS

Brown	GP147BR	½yd (45cm)

ROMAN GLASS

Brown	GP01BR	½yd (45cm)

GUINEA FLOWER

Brown	GP59BR	½yd (45cm)

GERBERA

Brown	PWKF06BR	½yd (45cm)

Light Fabrics
SHARKS TEETH

Brown	BM60BR	½yd (45cm)

ABORIGINAL DOT

Ocean	GP71ON	¼yd (25cm)
Forest	GP71FO	⅜yd (40cm)

PAPERWEIGHT

Sludge	GP20SL	⅜yd (40cm)

CURLIQUE

Grey	PJ87GY	½yd (45cm)
Ochre	PJ87OC	¼yd (25cm)

Backing Fabric
JAPANESE CHRYSANTHEMUM

Antique	PJ41AN	5½yd (5m)

Batting
78in x 93in (198cm x 236cm)

Binding
SPOT

Brown	GP70BR	⅝yd (60cm)

Quilting Thread
Toning machine quilting thread

TEMPLATES

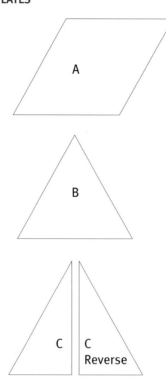

PATCHES
This classic Tumbling Blocks pattern is made the easy way by splitting the top of each tumbling block into 2 triangles, then piecing the quilt in vertical rows. It is made using a 120-degree diamond patch (Template A), an equilateral triangle (Template B), and a right-angled triangle to fill the column ends (Template C and C Reverse).

CUTTING OUT
Remove all selvedges before cutting out fabric. Cut the patches with the fabric right side up and not doubled.

Diamonds (Template A)
Cut 4in (10.2cm) strips across the width of the fabric. Each strip will give you 8 diamonds per width of fabric. You will need a total of 280. Place the template on the fabric strip as shown in the Cutting Patches Diagram.

Cut 62 in GP92DK; 37 in GP71OD; 29 in GP70BK and PJ87GY; 28 in GP92AN; 25 in BM60BR; 18 in GP71FO and GP20SL; 12 in PJ87OC and GP147BK and 10 in GP71ON.

Triangles (Template B)
Cut 4⅜in (11.1cm) strips across the width of the fabric. Each strip will give you 15 triangles per full width of fabric. You will need a total of 280. Place the template on the fabric strip, rotating it 180 degrees alternately, as shown in the Cutting Patches Diagram.
Cut 58 in PWKF06BR and GP147BR; 48 in GP59BR; 36 in BM53OC and GP01BR; 20 in GP71CC; 24 in GP92AN.

Half Triangles (Template C and C Reverse)
From GP147BK cut 2 strips 4¾in (12cm) x width of fabric. Cut 20 shapes using Template C and 20 using Template C Reverse. Keep the shapes in two separate piles.

Backing
Cut PJ41AN in half across the width to form two pieces.

Binding
In GP70BR cut 9 strips 2½in (6.4cm) across the width of the fabric.

MAKING THE QUILT
Use a ¼in (6mm) seam allowance throughout. Lay out the whole quilt as shown in the Quilt Assembly Diagram, forming 20 vertical columns. Take great care to place the dark, medium and light fabrics in the correct positions – a design wall will help with this. When laying out the patches, try to place each one so that the straight grain ends up on the outside edges of each row. This will help prevent stretching when the patches are sewn. Taking a photo of the design-wall arrangement will be a useful reference when sewing the vertical columns together.
Piece the columns together one at a time (see Piecing Patches Diagram), ending with a C or C Reverse template at the top and bottom of the column. Now sew the columns together.

CUTTING PATCHES DIAGRAM

Diamonds

4in
(10.2cm)

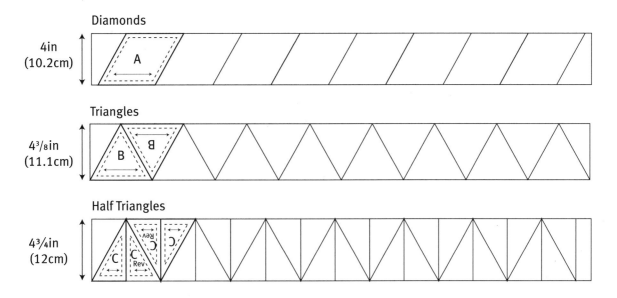

Triangles

4³/₈in
(11.1cm)

Half Triangles

4³/₄in
(12cm)

PIECING PATCHES DIAGRAM

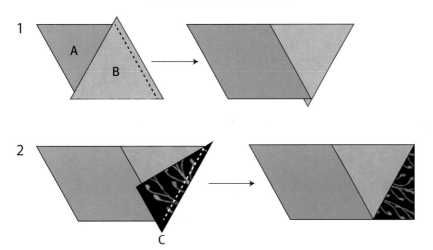

1

A   B

2

C

FINISHING THE QUILT

Press the quilt top. Sew the backing pieces together using a ¼in (6mm) seam allowance and trim to form a piece approx. 78in x 95in (198cm x 241cm). Press the seam open.

Layer the quilt top, batting and backing and baste together (see page 164).

Quilt as preferred. The quilt shown was quilted in the ditch around each hexagon block and also ½in (1.3cm) inside each hexagon.

Trim quilt edges and attach the binding (see page 165).

DARK FABRICS	MEDIUM FABRICS	LIGHT FABRICS
GP71OD	GP71CC	BM60BR
GP92DK	GP92AN	GP71ON
GP147BK	BM53OC	GP71FO
GP70BK	GP147BR	GP20SL
	GP01BR	PJ87GY
	GP59BR	PJ87OC
	PWKF06BR	

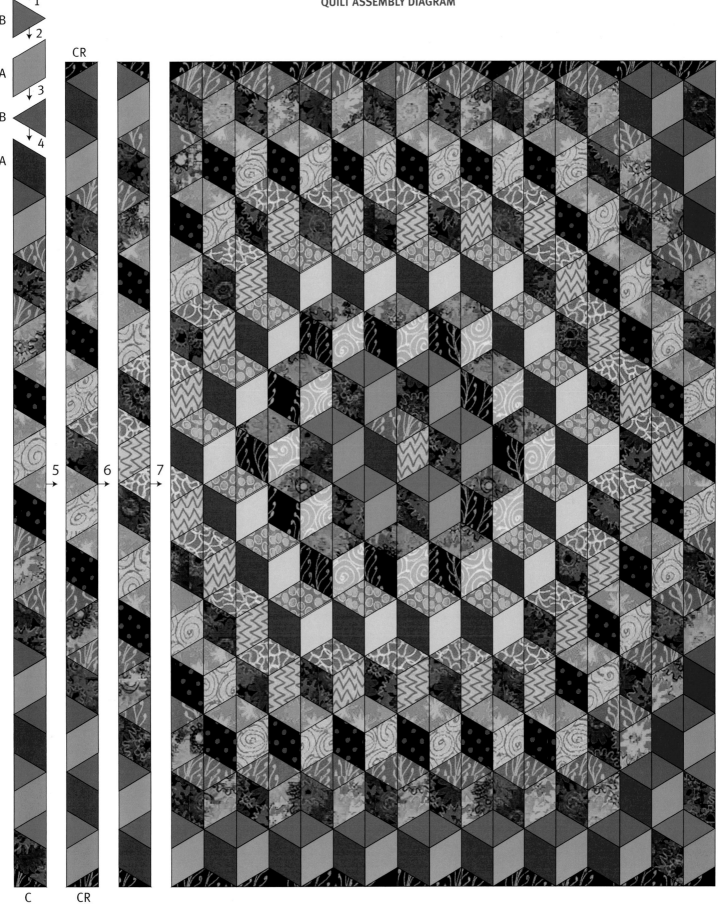

starburst ***

Kaffe Fassett

The Lone Star Quilt is a very traditional design and is still popular today. The inspiration for this quilt was taken from a pretty, pastel Lone Star quilt (see page 13) made from printed cotton fabrics. The quilt described here is made in the traditional way by sewing individual diamond patches together into larger diamond segments. The segments are sewn to the background squares and triangles using Y-seams.

The outer sections of the star are infilled with large squares and triangles.

CUTTING OUT
Remove all selvedges before cutting out fabric.

SIZE OF FINISHED QUILT
86in x 86in (218.5cm x 218.5cm)

MATERIALS
Fabrics calculated at minimum width of fabric approx. 40in (101.6cm), unless otherwise stated.

Patchwork Fabrics
MAD PLAID
Pastel	BM37PT	½yd (45cm)

JUMBLE
Candy	BM53CD	½yd (45cm)

MILLEFIORE
Pastel	GP92PT	½yd (45cm)
Pink	GP92PK	⅜yd (40cm)

PAPERWEIGHT
Lime	GP20LM	⅜yd (40cm)

ZIG ZAG
Yellow	BM43YE	¼yd (25cm)

GUINEA FLOWER
Grey	GP59GY	¼yd (25cm)
Brown	GP59BR	¼yd (25cm)
Yellow	GP59YE	¼yd (25cm)

BRASSICA
Moss	PJ51MS	¾yd (70cm)

JUPITER
Pastel	GP131PT	⅜yd (40cm)

SPOT
Turquoise	GP70TQ	¾yd (70cm)

ARTISAN SQUIGGLE
Pink	PWKF05PK	⅜yd (40cm)

ROMAN GLASS
Pink	GPO1PK	¾yd (70cm)
Gold	GP01GD	4½yd (4.2m)

Backing Fabric
JAPANESE CHRYSANTHEMUM
Spring	PJ41SP	6¾yd (6.2m)

Batting
95in x 95in (241.5cm x 241.5cm)

Binding
SPOT
Lavender	GP70LV	¾yd (70cm)

Quilting Thread
Machine quilting thread

TEMPLATE

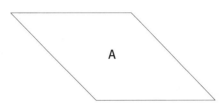

A

PATCHES
The central star shape is made from one small diamond patch (Template A). The 64 small diamonds are sewn together into a larger diamond-shaped segment, with 8 of these needed in total to create the star.

Background Squares and Triangles
Cut the background squares and triangles from GP01GD before you cut any diamonds from this fabric. Lone Star blocks are tricky to make to an exact size, so although the sizes given here are exact, *we strongly advise cutting the patches larger.* Check them against your own quilt once the segments have been joined together and trim down if needed. Cut 4 background squares 25¾in x 25¾in (65.4cm x 65.4cm).
Cut a 37⅛in x 37⅛in (94.3cm x 94.3cm) square. Cut this square diagonally both ways to make 4 triangles.

CUTTING DIAMONDS DIAGRAM

Folded fabric

Selvedge

Right side

A

Wrong side

Selvedge

Diamond 1   Diamond 2

DIAMONDS SEGMENTS DIAGRAM

Diamond 1
Diamond 2

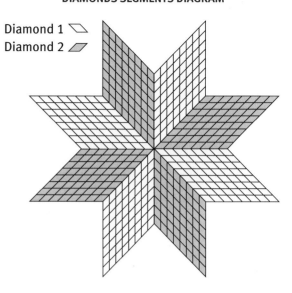

Diamonds

Use Template A to cut the small diamonds, cutting along the width of the fabric, with the grainline arrow as shown in the Cutting Diamonds Diagram. Cut the strips 6in (15.2cm) x width of fabric and press in half, wrong sides together, so the depth is 3in (7.6cm). Trim the fold off the doubled fabric so that the strip measures 2¾in (7cm). Cutting the diamonds with the fabric doubled in this way means that two diamonds are cut at once – one facing one way (Diamond 1) and the other facing the opposite way (Diamond 2). This will ensure that the fabric grain of the patches is always on the straight grain, not the bias. The Diamond Segments Diagram shows where these two diamonds are used in the star pattern.

Cut the following numbers of diamonds – remember that you will end up with twice the numbers given as you are cutting through doubled fabric. When cut, separate the diamonds into two piles – Pile 1 and Pile 2 (256 diamonds in each pile).

Cut 24 in BM37PT; 20 in BM53CD; 24 in GP92PT; 16 in GP92PK; 12 in GP20LM; 8 in BM43YE; 4 in GP59GY; 4 in GP59BR; 8 in GP59YE; 28 in PJ51MS; 16 in GP131PT; 32 in GP70TQ; 12 in PWKF05PK; 28 in GP01PK; 20 in GP01GD.

Backing

From PJ41SP cut 2 lengths approx. 95in (241.5cm) long. From the remaining piece, cut 2 strips 50in (127cm) long x 16in (40.6cm) wide.

Binding

From GP70SG, cut 10 strips 2½in (6.4cm) across the width. Sew together end to end.

MAKING THE LARGE DIAMOND SEGMENTS

All 8 segments are made in the same way and with the same fabric pattern, but use the Pile 1 diamonds for 4 of the segments and the Pile 2 diamonds for the other 4 segments. Use a ¼in (6mm) seam allowance throughout. Each segment has 64 diamonds. Lay one segment out in the pattern shown in the Segment Assembly Diagram. Sew together in rows and then sew the rows together.

Repeat to make all 8 segments.

DIAMONDS ASSEMBLY DIAGRAM

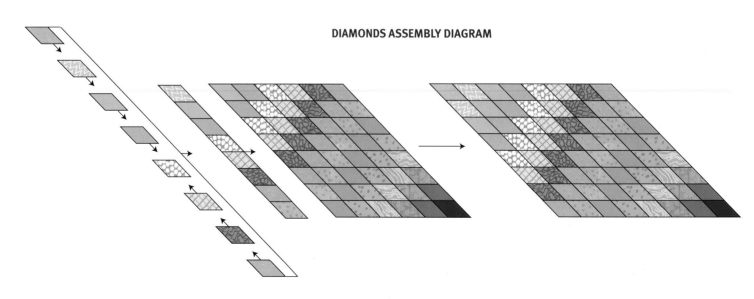

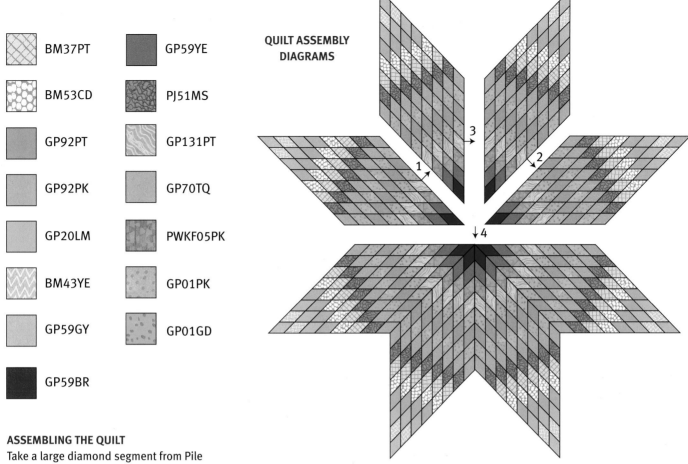 BM37PT	GP59YE		

BM37PT

BM53CD

GP92PT

GP92PK

GP20LM

BM43YE

GP59GY

GP59BR

GP59YE

PJ51MS

GP131PT

GP70TQ

PWKF05PK

GP01PK

GP01GD

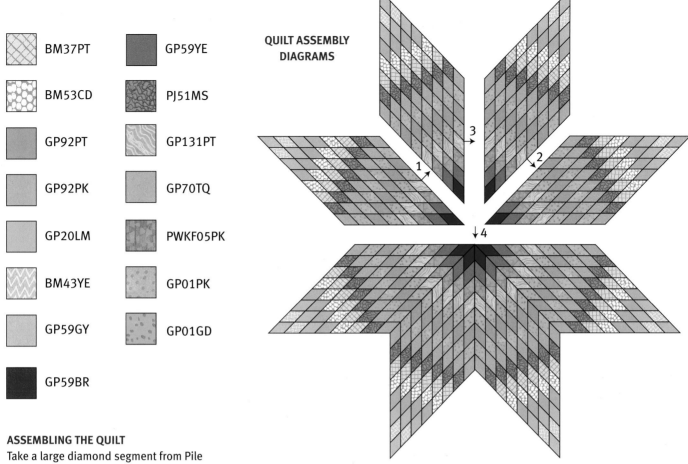

QUILT ASSEMBLY DIAGRAMS

ASSEMBLING THE QUILT

Take a large diamond segment from Pile 1 and a segment from Pile 2 and join together, stopping ¼in (6mm) from the outside edge of the star shape. Press the seam open. Repeat with three more pairs. Sew the top 2 pairs together, stopping ¼in (6mm) from the outside edge. Sew the bottom 2 pairs together in the same way. Join the 2 halves of the star together (see Quilt Assembly Diagram). Now insert the background corner squares and the background triangles using Y-seams.

FINISHING THE QUILT

Press the quilt top. Using a ¼in (6mm) seam allowance, sew the 2 narrow strips of backing fabric together end to end and trim to measure 95in (241.5cm) long. Sew this narrow panel between the 2 wider pieces to form a backing approx. 95in x 95in (241.5cm x 241.5cm). Layer the quilt top, batting and backing and baste together (see page 164). Quilt as preferred. The quilt shown was quilted in the ditch along the lines of the diamond segments. Parallel lines about 2¼in (5.7cm) apart were quilted in the corner squares and inset triangles. Trim the quilt edges and attach the binding (see page 165).

151

templates

Refer to the individual quilt instructions for the templates needed. Look for the quilt name on the templates, to make sure you are using the correct shapes for the project. Arrows on templates should be lined up with the straight grain of the fabric, which runs either along the selvedge or at 90 degrees to the selvedge. Following marked grain lines is important to avoid bias edges, which can cause distortion.

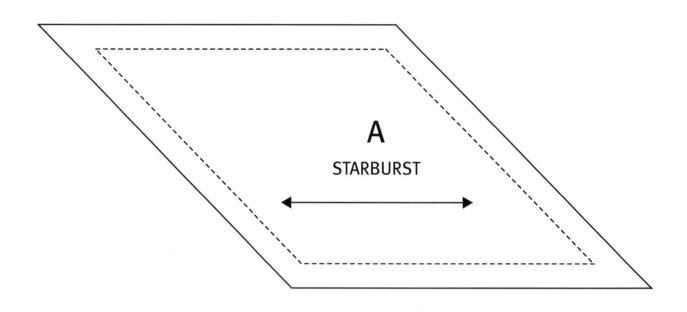

A

STARBURST

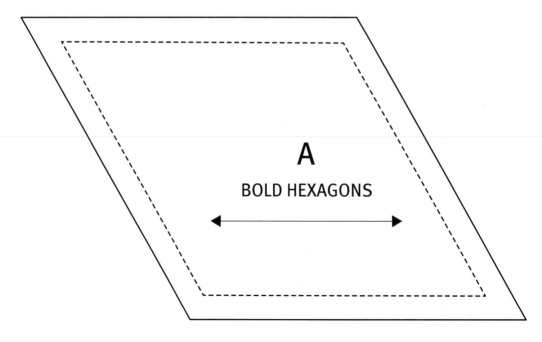

A

BOLD HEXAGONS

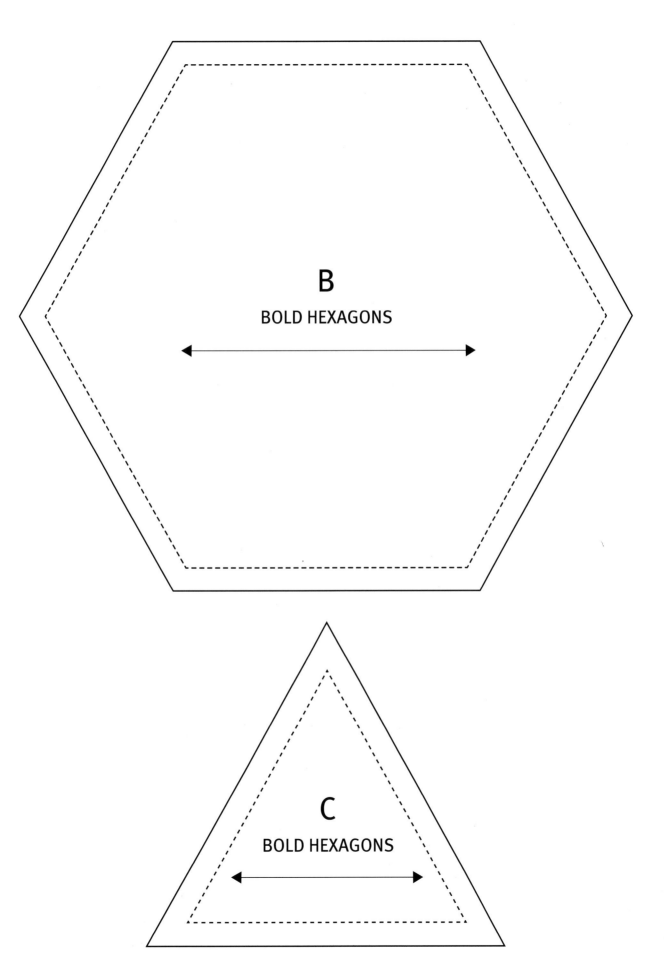

B

BOLD HEXAGONS

C

BOLD HEXAGONS

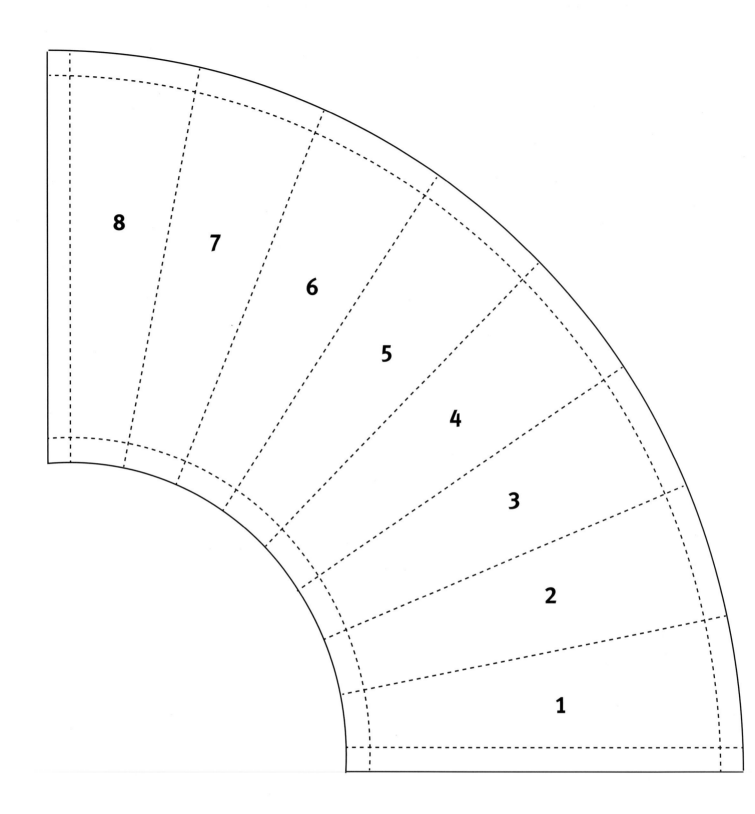

FOUNDATION PAPER PATTERN

DOTTY FANS

Pattern is reversed so it is ready to use

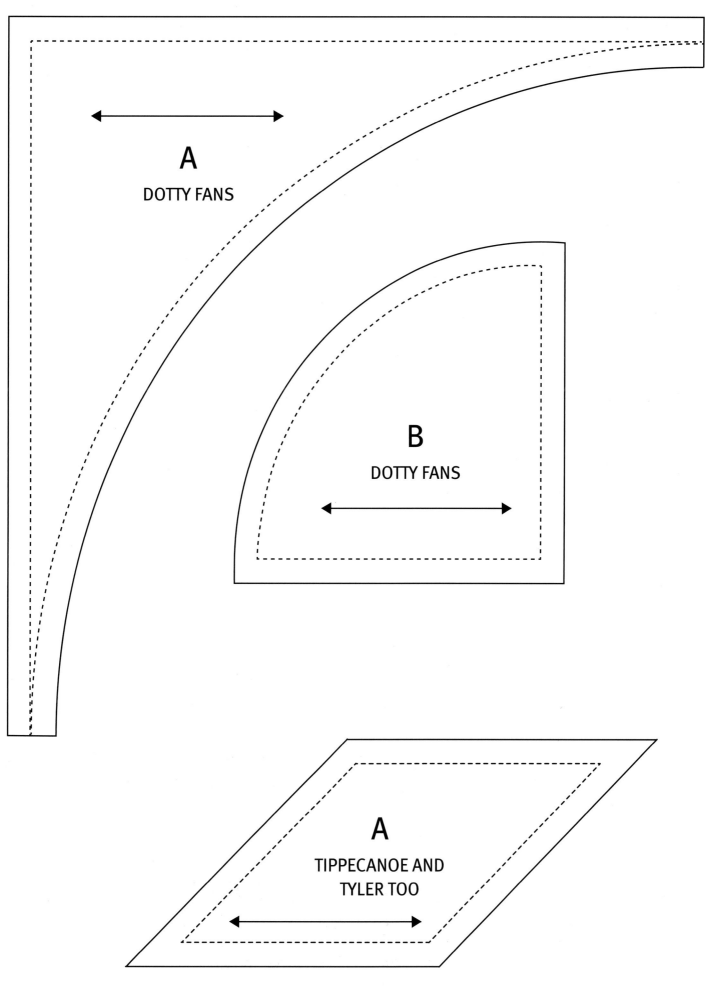

A
DOTTY FANS

B
DOTTY FANS

A
TIPPECANOE AND
TYLER TOO

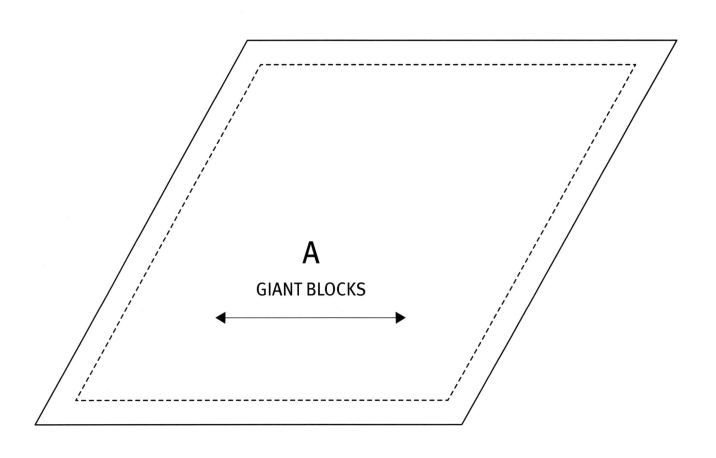

A

GIANT BLOCKS

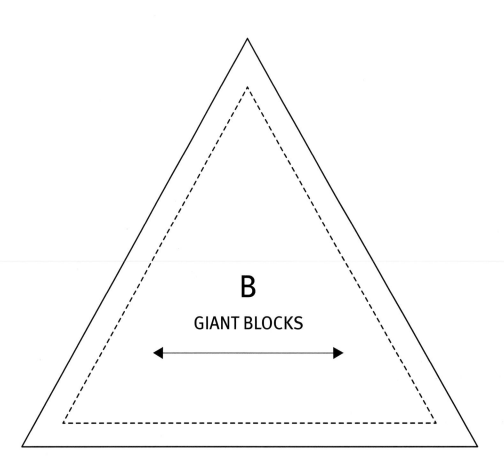

B

GIANT BLOCKS

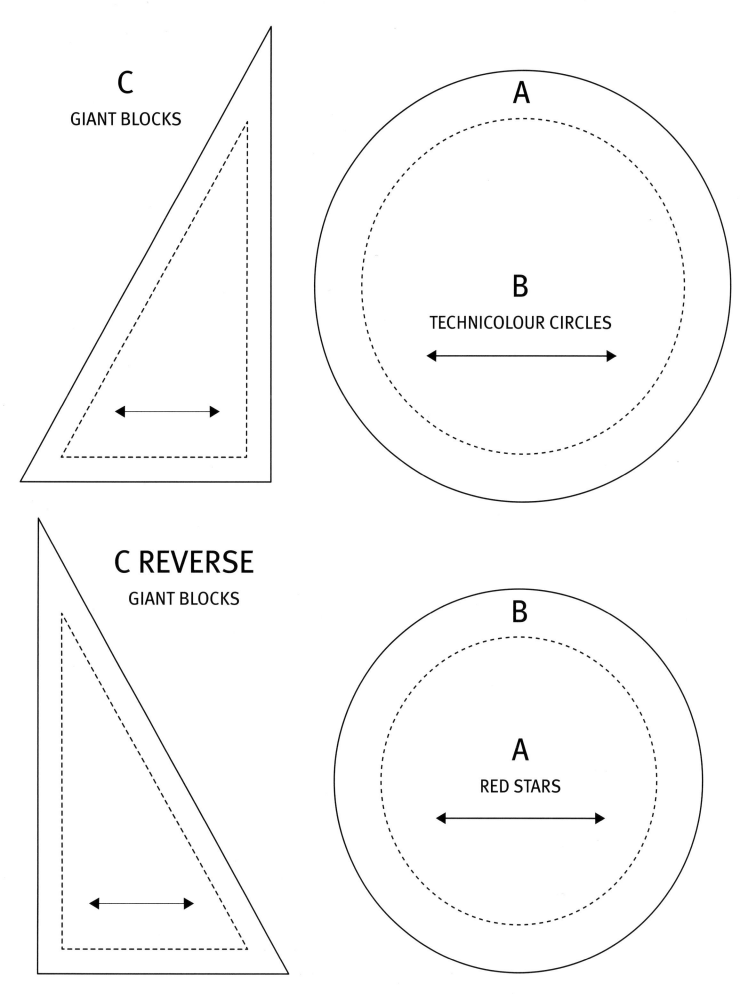

C
GIANT BLOCKS

A

B
TECHNICOLOUR CIRCLES

C REVERSE
GIANT BLOCKS

B

A
RED STARS

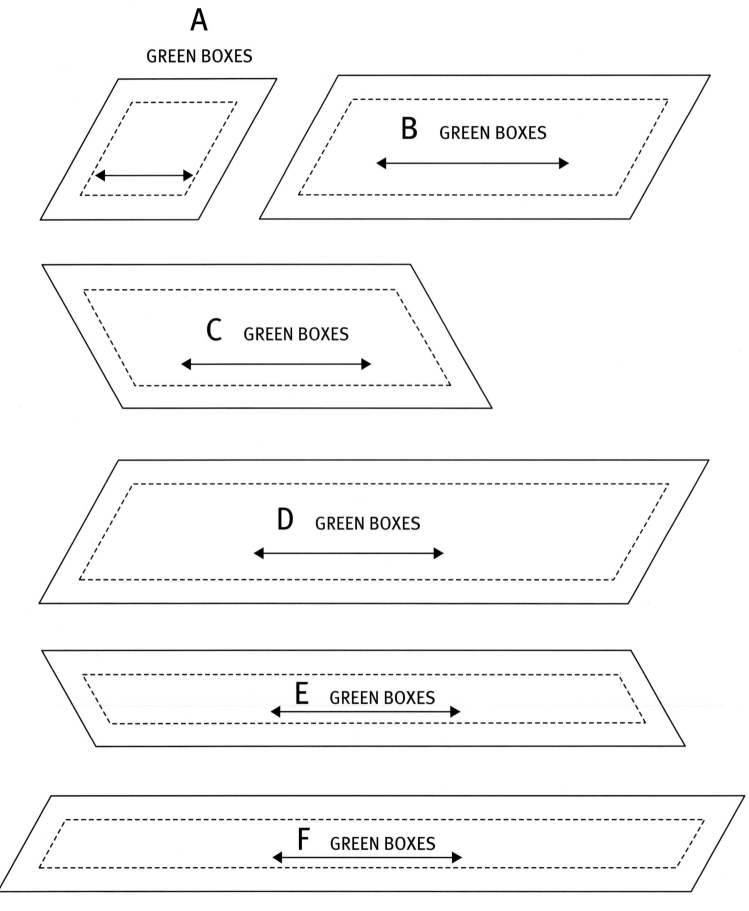

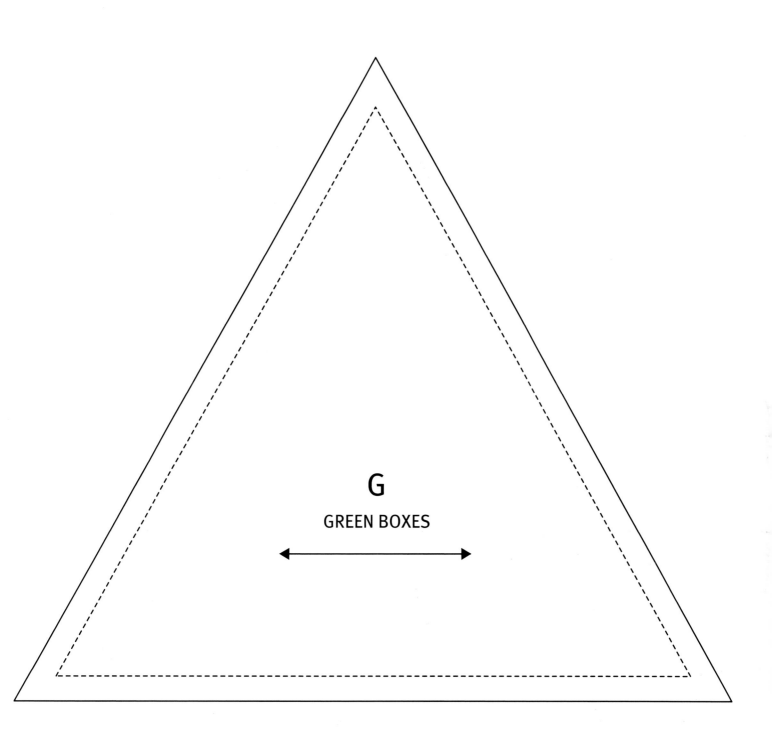

G

GREEN BOXES

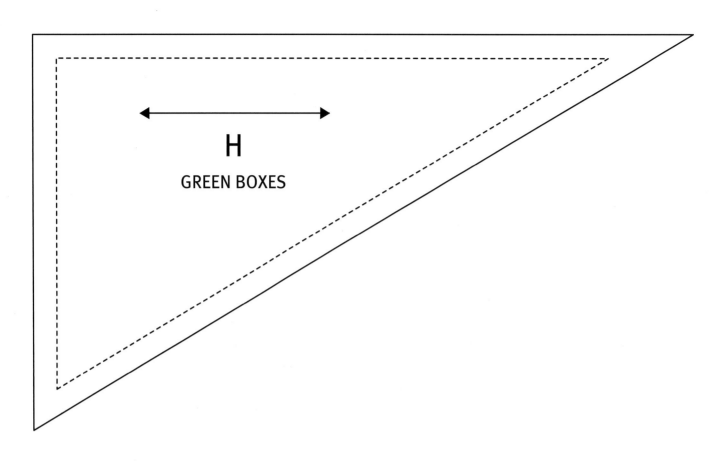

H
GREEN BOXES

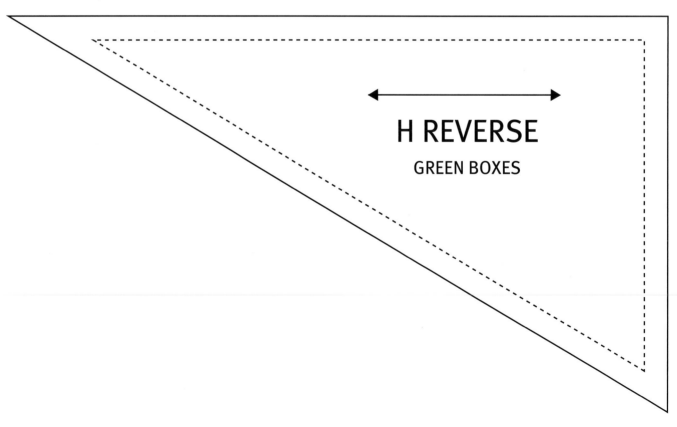

H REVERSE
GREEN BOXES

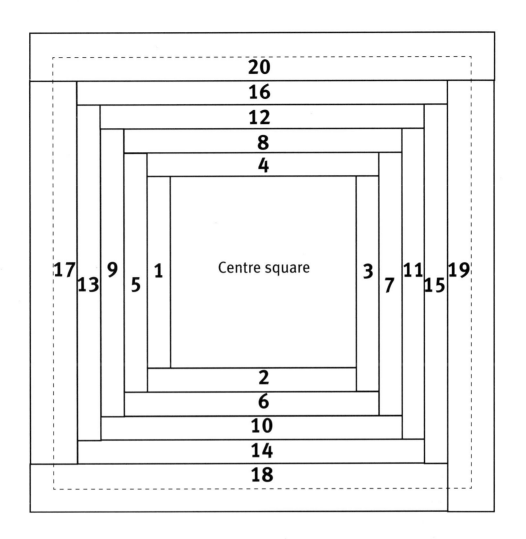

FOUNDATION PAPER PATTERN

BADGE OF HONOUR

Pattern is reversed so it is ready to use

patchwork know-how

These instructions are intended for the novice quilt maker, providing the basic information needed to make the projects in this book, along with some useful tips.

EXPERIENCE RATINGS
* Easy, straightforward, suitable for a beginner.
** Suitable for the average patchwork and quilter.
*** For the more experienced patchwork and quilter.

ABOUT THE FABRICS
The fabrics used for the quilts in this book are mainly from Kaffe Fassett Collective:
GP is the code for Kaffe Fassett's designs, **PJ** for Philip Jacobs' and **BM** for Brandon Mably's. The other fabrics used are Kaffe Fassett's Sew Artisan. The prefix PWKF is for the prints and the prefix PWBK is for the batiks.

PREPARING THE FABRIC
Prewash all new fabrics before you begin, to ensure that there will be no uneven shrinkage and no bleeding of colours when the finished quilt is laundered. Press the fabric whilst it is still damp to return crispness to it. All fabric requirements in this book are calculated on a 40in (101.5cm) usable fabric width, to allow for shrinkage and selvedge removal.

MAKING TEMPLATES
Transparent template plastic is the best material to use: it is durable and allows you to see the fabric and select certain motifs. You can also use thin stiff cardboard.

Templates for machine piecing
1 Trace off the actual-sized template provided either directly on to template plastic, or tracing paper, and then on to thin cardboard. Use a ruler to help you trace off the straight cutting line, dotted seam line and grain lines.

Sometimes templates are too large to print complete. Transfer the template onto the fold of a large sheet of paper, cut out and open out for the full template.
2 Cut out the traced off template using a craft knife, a ruler and a self-healing cutting mat.
3 Punch holes in the corners of the template, at each point on the seam line, using a hole punch.

Templates for hand piecing
• Make a template as for machine piecing, but do not trace off the cutting line. Use the dotted seam line as the outer edge of the template.

• This template allows you to draw the seam lines directly on to the fabric. The seam allowances can then be cut by eye around the patch.

CUTTING THE FABRIC
On the individual instructions for each project, you will find a summary of all the patch shapes used.

Always mark and cut out any border and binding strips first, followed by the largest patch shapes and finally the smallest ones, to make the most efficient use of your fabric. The border and binding strips are best cut using a rotary cutter.

Rotary cutting
Rotary cut strips are usually cut across the fabric from selvedge to selvedge, but some projects may vary, so please read through all the instructions before you start cutting the fabrics.

1 Before beginning to cut, press out any folds or creases in the fabric. If you are cutting a large piece of fabric, you will need to fold it several times to fit the cutting mat. When there is only a single fold, place the fold facing you. If the fabric is too wide to be folded only once, fold it concertina-style until it fits your mat. A small rotary cutter with a sharp blade will cut up to six layers of fabric; a large cutter up to eight layers.

2 To ensure that your cut strips are straight and even, the folds must be placed exactly parallel to the straight edges of the fabric and along a line on the cutting mat.

3 Place a plastic ruler over the raw edge of the fabric, overlapping it about ½in (1.25cm). Make sure the ruler is at right angles to both the straight edges and the fold to ensure that you cut along the straight grain. Press down on the ruler and wheel the cutter away from you along the edge of the ruler.

4 Open out the fabric to check the edge. Don't worry if it's not perfectly straight – a little wiggle will not show when the quilt is stitched together. Re-fold fabric, then place the ruler over the trimmed edge, aligning the edge with the markings on the ruler that match the correct strip width. Cut strip along the edge of the ruler.

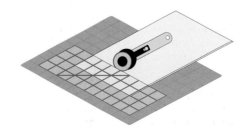

USING TEMPLATES
The most efficient way to cut out templates is by first rotary cutting a strip of fabric to the width stated for your template, and then marking off your templates along the strip, edge to edge at the required angle. This method leaves hardly any waste and gives a random effect to your patches.

A less efficient method is to fussy cut them, where the templates are cut individually by placing them on particular motifs or stripes, to create special effects. Although this method is more wasteful, it yields very interesting results.

1 Place the template face down, on the wrong side of the fabric, with the grain-line arrow following the straight grain of the fabric, if indicated. Be careful though – check with your individual instructions, as some instructions may ask you to cut patches on varying grains.

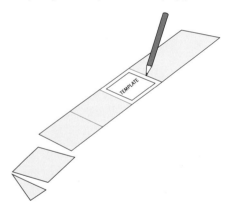

2 Hold the template firmly in place and draw around it with a sharp pencil or crayon, marking in the corner dots or seam lines. To save fabric, position patches close together or even touching. Don't worry if outlines positioned on the straight grain when drawn on striped fabrics do not always match the stripes when cut – this will add a degree of visual excitement to the patchwork!

3 Once you've drawn all the pieces needed, you are ready to cut the fabric, with either a rotary cutter and ruler or a pair of sharp sewing scissors.

BASIC HAND AND MACHINE PIECING
Patches can be stitched together by hand or machine. Machine stitching is quicker, but hand assembly allows you to carry your patches around with you and work on them in every spare moment. The choice is yours. For techniques that are new to you, practise on scrap pieces of fabric until you feel confident.

Machine piecing

Follow the quilt instructions for the order in which to piece the individual patchwork blocks and then assemble the blocks together in rows.

1 Seam lines are not marked on the fabric for simple shapes, so stitch ¼in (6mm) seams using the machine needle plate, a ¼in (6mm) wide machine foot, or tape stuck to the machine as a guide. Pin two patches with right sides together, matching edges.

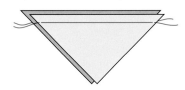

For some shapes, particularly diamonds, you need to match the sewing lines, not the fabric edges. Place 2 diamonds right sides together but offset so that the sewing lines intersect at the correct position. Use pins to secure for sewing.

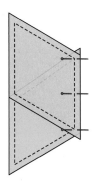

Set your machine at 10–12 stitches per inch (2.5cm) and stitch seams from edge to edge, removing pins as you feed the fabric through the machine.

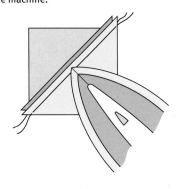

2 Press the seams of each patchwork block to one side before attempting to join it to another block. When joining diamond shaped blocks you will need to offset the blocks in the same way as diamond shaped patches, matching the sewing lines, not the fabric edges.

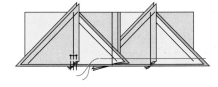

3 When joining rows of blocks, make sure that adjacent seam allowances are pressed in opposite directions to reduce bulk and make matching easier. Pin pieces together directly through the stitch line and to the right and left of the seam. Remove pins as you sew. Continue pressing seams to one side as you work.

Hand piecing

1 Pin two patches with right sides together, so that the marked seam lines are facing outwards.

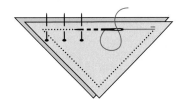

2 Using a single strand of strong thread, secure the corner of a seam line with a couple of back stitches.

3 Sew running stitches along the marked line, working 8–10 stitches per inch (2.5cm) and ending at the opposite seam line corner with a few back stitches. When hand piecing never stitch over the seam allowances.

4 Press the seams to one side, as shown in machine piecing (Step 2).

MACHINE APPLIQUÉ WITH ADHESIVE WEB

To make appliqué very easy you can use adhesive web (which comes attached to a paper backing sheet) to bond the motifs to the background fabric. There are two types of web available: the first keeps the pieces in place while they are stitched, the second permanently attaches the pieces so that no sewing is required. Follow steps 1 and 2 for the non-sew type and steps 1–3 for the type that requires sewing.

1 Trace the reversed appliqué design onto the paper side of the adhesive web, leaving a ¼in (6mm) gap between all the shapes. Roughly cut out the motifs ⅛in (3mm) outside your drawn line.

2 Bond the motifs to the reverse of your chosen fabrics. Cut out on the drawn line with very sharp scissors. Remove the backing paper by scoring the centre of the motif carefully with a scissor point and peeling the paper away from the centre out (to prevent damage to the edges). Place the motifs onto the background, noting any which may be layered. Cover with a clean cloth and bond with a hot iron (check instructions for temperature setting as adhesive web can vary depending on the manufacturer).

3 Using a contrasting or toning coloured thread in your machine, work small close zig zag stitches (or a blanket stitch if your machine has one) around the edge of the motifs; the majority of the stitching should sit on the appliqué shape. When stitching up to points stop with the machine needle in the down position, lift the foot of your machine, pivot the work, lower the foot and continue to stitch. Make sure all the raw edges are stitched.

HAND APPLIQUÉ

Good preparation is essential for speedy and accurate hand appliqué. The finger-pressing method is suitable for needle-turning application, used for simple shapes like leaves and flowers. Using a card template is the best method for bold simple motifs such as circles.

Finger–pressing method

1 To make your template, transfer the appliqué design using carbon paper on to stiff card, and cut out the template. Trace around the outline of your appliquéd shape on to the right side of your fabric using a well sharpened pencil. Cut out shapes, adding by eye a ¼in (6mm) seam allowance all around.

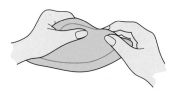

2 Hold the shape right side up and fold under the seam, turning along your drawn line, pinch to form a crease. Dampening the fabric makes this very easy. When using shapes with points such as leaves, turn in the seam allowance at the point first, as shown in the diagram. Then continue all round the shape. If your shapes have sharp curves, you can snip the seam allowance to ease the curve. Take care not to stretch the appliqué shapes as you work.

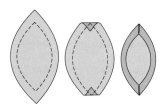

Straight stems

Place fabric face down and simply press over the ¼in (6mm) seam allowance along each edge. You don't need to finish the ends of stems that are layered under other appliqué shapes. Where the end of the stem is visible, simply tuck under the end and finish neatly.

Needle-turning application

Take the appliqué shape and pin in position. Stroke the seam allowance under with the tip of the needle as far as the creased pencil line, and hold securely in place with your thumb. Using a matching thread, bring the needle up from the back of the block into the edge of the shape and proceed to blind-hem in place. (This stitch allows the motifs to appear to be held on invisibly.) To do this, bring the thread out from below through the folded edge of the motif, never on the top. The stitches must be small, even and close together to prevent the seam allowance from unfolding and from frayed edges appearing. Try to avoid pulling the stitches too tight, as this will cause the motifs to pucker up. Work around the whole shape, stroking under each small section before sewing.

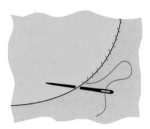

QUILTING

When you have finished piecing your patchwork and added any borders, press it carefully. It is now ready for quilting.

Marking quilting designs and motifs

Many tools are available for marking quilting patterns, check the manufacturer's instructions for use and test on scraps of fabric from your project. Use an acrylic ruler for marking straight lines.

Stencils

Some designs require stencils, these can be made at home, by transferring the designs on to template plastic, or stiff cardboard. The design is then cut away in the form of long dashes, to act as guides for both internal and external lines. These stencils are a quick method for producing an identical set of repeated designs.

BACKING FABRIC

The quilts in this book use two different widths of backing fabric – the standard width of 44in (112cm) and a wider one of 108in (274cm). If you can't find (or don't want to use) the wider fabric then select a standard-width fabric instead and adjust the amount accordingly. For most of the quilts in the book, using a standard-width fabric will probably mean joins in the fabric. The material list for each quilt assumes that an extra 4in of backing fabric is needed all round (8in in total) when making up the quilt sandwich, to allow for long-arm quilting if needed. We have assumed a usable width of 40in (102cm), to allow for selvedge removal and possible shrinkage after washing.

Preparing the backing and batting

• Remove the selvedges and piece together the backing fabric to form a backing at least 4in (10cm) larger all around than the patchwork top.

• Choose a fairly thin batting, preferably pure cotton, to give your quilt a flat appearance. If your batting has been rolled up, unroll it and let it rest before cutting it to the same size as the backing.

• For a large quilt it may be necessary to join two pieces of batting to fit. Lay the pieces of batting on a flat surface so that they overlap by around 8in (20cm). Cut a curved line through both layers.

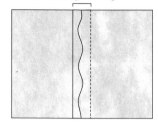

overlap wadding

• Carefully peel away the two narrow pieces and discard. Butt the curved cut edges back together. Stitch the two pieces together using a large herringbone stitch.

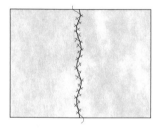

BASTING THE LAYERS TOGETHER

1 On the floor or on a large work surface, lay out the backing with wrong side uppermost. Use weights along the edges to keep it taut.

2 Lay the batting on the backing and smooth it out gently. Next lay the patchwork top, right side up, on top of the batting and smooth gently until there are no wrinkles. Pin at the corners and at the midpoints of each side, close to the edges.

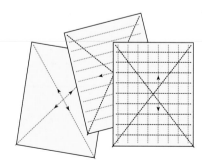

3 Beginning at the centre, baste diagonal lines outwards to the corners, making your stitches about 3in (7.5cm) long. Then, again starting at the centre, baste horizontal and vertical lines out to the edges. Continue basting until you have basted a grid of lines about 4in (10cm) apart over the entire quilt.

4 For speed, when machine quilting, some quilters prefer to baste their quilt sandwich layers together using rust-proof safety pins, spaced at 4in (10cm) intervals over the entire quilt.

HAND QUILTING

This is best done with the quilt mounted on a quilting frame or hoop, but as long as you have basted the quilt well, a frame is not essential. With the quilt top facing upwards, begin at the centre of the quilt and make even running stitches following the design. It is more important to make even stitches on both sides of the quilt than to make small ones. Start and finish your stitching with back stitches and bury the ends of your threads in the batting.

TIED QUILTING

If you prefer you could use tied quilting rather than machine quilting. For tied quilting, use a strong thread that will withstand being pulled through the quilt layers and tied in a knot. You can tie with the knot on the front of the quilt or the back, as preferred. Leaving tufts of thread gives an attractive, rustic look.

Thread a needle with a suitable thread, using the number of strands noted in the project. Put the needle and thread through from the front of the work, leaving a long tail. Go through to the back of the quilt, make a small stitch and then come back through to the front. Tie the threads together using a reef knot and trim the thread ends to the desired length. For extra security, you could tie a double knot or add a spot of fabric glue on the knot.

MACHINE QUILTING

• For a flat looking quilt, always use a walking foot on your machine for stitching straight lines, and a darning foot for free-motion quilting.

• It is best to start your quilting at the centre of the quilt and work out towards the borders, doing the straight quilting lines first (stitch-in-the-ditch) followed by the free-motion quilting.

• When free-motion quilting stitch in a loose meandering style as shown in the diagrams. Do not stitch too closely as this will make the quilt feel stiff when finished. If you wish you can include floral themes or follow shapes on the printed fabrics for added interest.

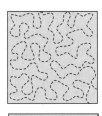

• Make it easier for yourself by handling the quilt properly. Roll up the excess quilt neatly to fit under your sewing machine arm, and use a table or chair to help support the weight of the quilt that hangs down the other side.

FINISHING

Preparing to bind the edges

Once you have quilted or tied your quilt sandwich together, remove all the basting stitches. Then, baste around the outer edge of the quilt ¼in (6mm) from the edge of the top patchwork layer. Trim the back and batting to the edge of the patchwork and straighten the edge of the patchwork if necessary.

Making the binding

1 Cut bias or straight grain strips the width required for your binding, making sure the grain-line is running the correct way on your straight grain strips. Cut enough strips until you have the required length to go around the edge of your quilt.

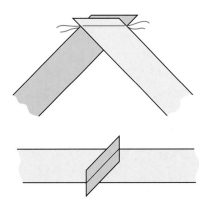

2 To join strips together, the two ends that are to be joined must be cut at a 45 degree angle, as above. Stitch right sides together, trim turnings and press seam open.

Binding the edges

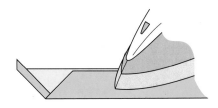

1 Cut the starting end of binding strip at a 45 degree angle, fold a ¼in (6mm) turning to wrong side along cut edge and press in place. With wrong sides together, fold strip in half lengthways, keeping raw edges level, and press.

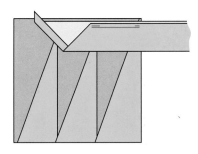

2 Starting at the centre of one of the long edges, place the doubled binding on to the right side of the quilt keeping raw edges level. Stitch the binding in place starting ¼in (6mm) in from the diagonal folded edge. Reverse stitch to secure, and work ¼in (6mm) in from edge of the quilt towards first corner of quilt. Stop ¼in (6mm) in from corner and work a few reverse stitches.

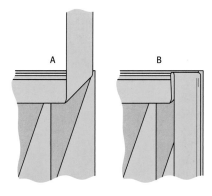

3 Fold the loose end of the binding up, making a 45 degree angle (see A). Keeping the diagonal fold in place, fold the binding back down, aligning the raw edges with the next side of the quilt. Starting at the point where the last stitch ended, stitch down the next side (see B).

4 Continue to stitch the binding in place around all the quilt edges in this way, tucking the finishing end of the binding inside the diagonal starting section.

5 Turn the folded edge of the binding on to the back of the quilt. Hand stitch the folded edge in place just covering binding machine stitches, and folding a mitre at each corner

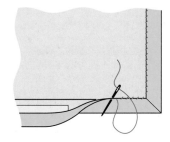

glossary of terms

Adhesive or fusible web This comes attached to a paper-backed sheet and is used to bond appliqué motifs to a background fabric. There are 2 types of web available, the first keeps the pieces in place whilst they are stitched, the second permanently attaches the pieces so that no sewing is required.

Appliqué The technique of stitching fabric shapes on to a background to create a design. It can be applied either by hand or machine with a decorative embroidery stitch, such as buttonhole, or satin stitch.

Backing The bottom layer of a quilt sandwich. It is made of fabric pieced to the size of the quilt top with the addition of about 4in (10.25cm) all around to allow for quilting take-up.

Basting or tacking This is a means of holding two fabric layers or the layers of a quilt sandwich together temporarily with large hand stitches or pins.

Batting or wadding This is the middle layer, or padding in a quilt. It can be made of cotton, wool, silk or synthetic fibres.

Bias The diagonal grain of a fabric. This is the direction which has the most give or stretch, making it ideal for bindings, especially on curved edges.

Binding A narrow strip of fabric used to finish off the edges of quilts or projects; it can be cut on the straight grain of a fabric or on the bias.

Block A single design unit that when stitched together with other blocks create the quilt top. It is most often a square, hexagon, or rectangle, but it can be any shape. It can be pieced or plain.

Border A frame of fabric stitched to the outer edges of the quilt top. Borders can be narrow or wide, pieced or plain. As well as making the quilt larger, they unify the overall design and draw attention to the central area.

Chalk pencils Available in various colours, they are used for marking lines or spots on fabric.

Cutting mat Designed for use with a rotary cutter, it is made from a special self-healing material that keeps your cutting blade sharp. Cutting mats come in various sizes and are usually marked with a grid to help you line up the edges of fabric and cut out larger pieces.

Design wall Used for laying out fabric patches before sewing. A large wall or folding board covered with flannel fabric or cotton batting in a neutral shade (dull beige or grey work well) will hold fabric in place so that an overall view can be taken of the placement.

Free-motion quilting Curved wavy quilting lines stitched in a random manner. Stitching diagrams are often given for you to follow as a loose guide.

Fussy cutting This is when a template is placed on a particular motif, or stripe, to obtain interesting effects. This method is not as efficient as strip cutting, but yields very interesting results.

Grain The direction in which the threads run in a woven fabric. In a vertical direction it is called the lengthwise grain, which has very little stretch. The horizontal direction, or crosswise grain is slightly stretchy, but diagonally the fabric has a lot of stretch. This grain is called the bias. Wherever possible the grain of a fabric should run in the same direction on a quilt block and borders.

Grain lines These are arrows printed on templates which should be aligned with the fabric grain.

Inset seams or setting-in A patchwork technique whereby one patch (or block) is stitched into a V-shape formed by the joining of two other patches (or blocks).

Patch A small shaped piece of fabric used in the making of a patchwork pattern.

Patchwork The technique of stitching small pieces of fabric (patches) together to create a larger piece of fabric, usually forming a design.

Pieced quilt A quilt composed of patches.

Quilting Traditionally done by hand with running stitches, but for speed modern quilts are often stitched by machine. The stitches are sewn through the top, wadding and backing to hold the three layers together. Quilting stitches are usually worked in some form of design, but they can be random.

Quilting hoop Consists of two wooden circular or oval rings with a screw adjuster on the outer ring. It stabilises the quilt layers, helping to create an even tension.

Reducing glass Used for viewing the complete composition of a quilt at a glance. It works like a magnifier in reverse. A useful tool for checking fabric placement before piecing a quilt.

Rotary cutter A sharp circular blade attached to a handle for quick, accurate cutting. It is a device that can be used to cut several layers of fabric at one time. It must be used in conjunction with a self-healing cutting mat and a thick plastic ruler.

Rotary ruler A thick, clear plastic ruler marked with lines in imperial or metric measurements. Sometimes they also have diagonal lines indicating 45 and 60 degree angles. A rotary ruler is used as a guide when cutting out fabric pieces using a rotary cutter.

Sashing A piece or pieced sections of fabric interspaced between blocks.

Sashing posts When blocks have sashing between them the corner squares are known as sashing posts.

Selvedges Also known as selvages, these are the firmly woven edges down each side of a fabric length. Selvedges should be trimmed off before cutting out your fabric, as they are more liable to shrink when the fabric is washed.

Stitch-in-the-ditch or Ditch quilting Also known as quilting-in-the-ditch. The quilting stitches are worked along the actual seam lines, to give a pieced quilt texture.

Template A pattern piece used as a guide for marking and cutting out fabric patches, or marking a quilting, or appliqué design. Usually made from plastic or strong card that can be reused many times. Templates for cutting fabric usually have marked grain lines which should be aligned with the fabric grain.

Threads One hundred percent cotton or cotton-covered polyester is best for hand and machine piecing. Choose a colour that matches your fabric. When sewing different colours and patterns together, choose a medium to light neutral colour, such as grey or ecru. Specialist quilting threads are available for hand and machine quilting.

Walking foot or Quilting foot This is a sewing machine foot with dual feed control. It is very helpful when quilting, as the fabric layers are fed evenly from the top and below, reducing the risk of slippage and puckering.

Yo-Yos A circle of fabric double the size of the finished puff is gathered up into a rosette shape.

Y-seams See Inset seams.

ACKNOWLEDGMENTS

Firstly, I would like to thank the American Museum in Bath, and Kate Hebert, the Curator, for making their wonderful antique quilts available to me as the cornerstone for this book.

My very grateful thanks to Liza and Janet, with their respective teams of makers*, for masterminding the piecing of these wonderful quilts. Special thanks to Liza and Drew, for hosting the location photography team and steering us towards so many brilliant locations (ably helped by Liz Dougherty), to Debbie Patterson for her ever-excellent photography and to Anne Wilson for her sensitive layouts.

We photographed in New Hope and Lumberville in PA, and in Lambertville, Frenchtown and Stockton in NJ, and are most grateful to those towns. In particular, we would like to thank the following: Sycamore Farm, Cuttalossa Farm, Rittenhouse Inn (Frenchtown NJ), Fred Gaspy, Colleen Maloney, Bruce and Coleen Dolmat, Kathy Hausman and Jim Hill, Concie and Dave Bassett-Cann, New Hope and Ivyland RR, and Sara Bizarro and Jordan Mokriski.

Last, but by no means least, I am indebted, as ever, to Brandon, for his invaluable perspective and support.

* Autumn (Bobbi Penniman)
  Badge of Honour (Julie Harvey)
  Bold Hexagons (Liza Prior Lucy)
  Coleus Columns (Liza Prior Lucy)
  Contrast Columns (Ilaria Padovani)
  Dark 9-Patch (Liza Prior Lucy)
  Dotty Fans (Ilaria Padovani)
  Giant Blocks (Julie Harvey)
  Green Boxes (Ilaria Padovani)
  Kites (Ilaria Padovani)
  Moonlight (Julie Harvey)
  Pastel 9-Patch (Liza Prior Lucy)
  Red Ribbons (Judy Baldwin)
  Red Stars (Ilaria Padovani)
  Sashed Baskets (Julie Harvey)
  Squares on Point (Mira Mayer)
  Starburst (Julie Harvey)
  Stonewall (Corienne Kramer)
  Technicolour Circles (Janet Haigh)
  Tippecanoe and Tyler Too (Liza Prior Lucy)

distributors and stockists

To find a retailer in the USA and Canada, please go to www.freespiritfabrics.com

For the following countries, see contact information below:

AUSTRALIA
XLN Fabrics
2/21 Binney Rd
Kings Park
NSW 2148
www.xln.com.au
email: allanmurphy@xln.com.au

CHINA (inc HONG KONG/MACAO/ TAIWAN)
Wan Mei Di China
502 CaoXi Rd (N)
Xuhui District
Shanghai
China
email: 12178550@qq.com

EUROPE (SEE UK/EUROPE)

HONG KONG
Wan Mei Di China
502 CaoXi Rd (N)
Xuhui District
Shanghai
China
email: 12178550@qq.com

JAPAN
Kiyohara & Co Ltd
4-5-2 Minamikyuhoji-machi Chuo-ku
Osaka 541-8506
www. kiyohara.co.jp
email: Kazuo.fujii@kiyohara.co.jp

KOREA
Young Do Trimart Co Ltd
6th floor Dongwon Building
458 Cheonggyecheon-ro
Seongdong-gu
Seoul
www.youndoco.tradekorea.com
email: Trade1@youngdo.co.kr

MACAO
Wan Mei Di China
502 CaoXi Rd (N)
Xuhui District
Shanghai
China
email: 12178550@qq.com

NEW ZEALAND
Fabco Ltd
280 School Road
Muriwai Valley 0881
www.fabco.co.nz
melanie@fabco.co.nz

SOUTH AFRICA
Arthur Bales Pty Ltd
62 4th Avenue
Johannesburg 2104
www.arthurbales.co.za
email: nicci@arthurbales.co.za

TAIWAN
Long Teh Trading Co Ltd
71 Hebei W. St
Tai Chung 40669
email: Longteh.quilt@gmail.com

Wan Mei Diy China
502 CaoXi Rd (N)
Xuhui District
Shanghai
China
email: 12178550@qq.com

UK/EUROPE
Rhinetex
Geurdeland 7
6673 DR Andelst
Netherlands
www.rhinetex.com
email: info@rhinetex.com

MEZ Gmbh
Kaiserstrasse 1
79341 Kenzingen
Germany
www.mezcrafts.de
email: kenzingen.vertrieb@ mezcrafts.com